LAW OF ATTRACTION AND MANIFESTATION LEARNING FROM NATURE

Mrs. Sonal Yadav

Dr. Rajpal

Mr. Surya Kant Swami

Dr. Kaushalendra

Dr. Naveen Kumar

Title   : Law of Attraction and Menifestation Learning from Nature

Author : Mrs. Sonal Yadav, Dr. Rajpal, Mr. Surya Kant Swami
         Dr. Kaushalendra, Dr. Naveen Kumar

Edition : First (December, 2024)

ISBN   : 9789348332219

Published by

PRACHI
DIGITAL PUBLICATION

Regd. Add.: 254, Khuriyakhatta No. 10, Bindukhatta,
Lalkuan, Nainital - 262402, Uttarakhand, India
Website : www.prachidigital.com
E-mail : info@prachidigital.in
Phone : +91 976041 7980, +91 976041 8103

Printed by :

Manipal Technologies Limited, Bengaluru - 560001, Karnataka

OUTLINE

CHAPTER 1

UNDERSTANDING THE LAW OF ATTRACTION

1.1 Law of Attraction: A Seed Planted in Time

The concept of Law of Attraction has intrigued and transformed lives over centuries by merging philosophical, psychological, and spiritual principles. To grasp it fully, one must delve into its roots and evolutionary journey. Its origins can be traced to ancient spiritual and philosophical traditions emphasizing the power of thoughts, beliefs, and intentions. Historically, numerous philosophers believed human consciousness could shape reality. This idea resonates with spiritual traditions suggesting that the universe operates as a flow of energies responding to internal thoughts and emotions, akin to how plants and trees rely on sunlight, water, and soil to flourish. The environment reflects this interplay, where each component, from the sun to the earth, contributes to the vitality and growth of organisms.

The 19th century marked a more defined emergence of Law of Attraction, primarily through the New Thought movement in the United States. This movement promoted the idea that reality could be altered via positive thinking and mental power. Influential figures such as Phineas Quimby and Ralph Waldo Emerson advocated that thoughts are not arbitrary but potent tools capable of shaping life experiences. Quimby asserted that modifying thoughts could alleviate suffering and create desired outcomes, paralleling the way environmental energies drive changes in nature. This mirrors how trees in a forest adapt to seasonal shifts, with each season bringing unique growth or shedding, much like thoughts influencing personal reality.

The 20th century saw Law of Attraction garner increasing recognition, particularly through works such as The Science of Getting Rich by Wallace D. Wattles and Think and Grow Richerer by Napoleon Hill. These books proposed that focused thinking and understanding universal laws could yield wealth and success. Hill emphasized the significance of having a definitive purpose, unwavering belief, and visualization to attract desired results. Both authors propagated notion mind could draw opportunities, akin to plants harnessing solar energy for growth. Just as flowers bloom by aligning with sunlight, individuals can achieve success by harmonizing their thoughts with goals and surrounding energies.

The popularity of Law of Attraction continued to soar in the 20th century, propelled by self-help literature and motivational speakers. Notably, Esther and Jerry Hicks gained prominence for their book Law of Attraction: The Basics of the Teachings of Abraham. They illustrated that "like attracts like," explaining that emotions and thoughts emit energies that draw taking or drawing energies of universe. This idea parallels the interconnectedness of natural elements, where their energy levels influence one another. For instance, wind disperses seeds to fertile grounds, enabling their growth; similarly, aligning thoughts with favorable energy can lead to opportunities. Their teachings underscored the importance of emotional well-being in attracting positive results, much like a thriving ecosystem fosters the prosperity of plants and wildlife.

In recent times, the mainstreaming of Law of Attraction has been amplified by social media and the wellness trend. The 2006 documentary The Secret introduced these concepts for a broader audience, blending personal anecdotes with expert insights to demonstrate the power of focused thoughts and intentions in manifesting dreams. This movement spurred a rise in workshops, courses, and coaching programs designed to help individuals apply Law of Attraction, mirroring the natural energy flows that foster growth and transformation. Just as nature thrives through the harmonious coexistence of its elements, Law of Attraction posits that people can achieve a balanced and fulfilling life by aligning with the right energies.

Despite its acclaim, Law of Attraction has its detractors. Critics argue it oversimplifies life's complexities and may lead individuals to neglect actionable steps required for success. They caution that reliance solely on positive thinking can result in unrealistic expectations and disappointment. Advocates, however, contend that Law of Attractionhave more than optimism-it necessitates a clear purpose, emotional alignment, and actionable steps toward goals. Like tending a seed that requires sunlight, water, and care to grow, achieving success demands consistent nurturing, with positive thoughts serving as one component of the broader process.

Understanding Law of Attractionhave acknowledging its psychological underpinnings. Cognitive-behavioral theories suggest that thoughts and beliefs significantly impact emotions and behaviors. By adopting positive thinking, individuals can alter their emotional state and actions, yielding favorable outcomes. This mirrors natural systems, where healthy soil produces robust plants, and a constructive mindset fosters positive experiences. Just as fertile soil is essential for optimal growth, a mind enriched with clear and positive thoughts is pivotal in crafting the desired life.

Additionally, Law of Attraction aligns with the concept that all entities, including thoughts and emotions, possess vibrational frequencies. This idea parallels natural principles, where energies and elements are interlinked. Elevating one's vibrational state through gratitude and love harmonizes desires with the universe's flow, akin to tuning a radio to the correct frequency. Harmony and balance, essential in nature, enable individuals to attract positive outputs by aligning internal energies with the universe. Practices like mindfulness and meditation reinforce this alignment, much like a tree's roots anchor it firmly, providing stability amidst changing conditions.

Exploring Law of Attraction reveals diverse techniques to unlock its potential. Visualization is the powerful method, allowing individuals to mentally envision achieving their objectives, aligning subconscious thoughts with conscious goals. This process clarifies purpose and fosters a stronger connection to ambitions, reinforcing belief in their attainability. Just as a gardener envisions a lush garden before planting, visualizing success lays the foundation for its realization. Similarly, affirmations-positive declarations that reshape thoughts-help replace limiting beliefs with empowering ones.

Community also plays a essential role in applying Law of Attraction. Supportive environments, such as workshops or online groups, offer inspiration and encouragement, helping individuals stay committed to their manifestation journeys. Sharing experiences fosters a sense of connection and belonging, much like trees in a forest supporting one another through their interconnected roots, ensuring collective strength and nourishment.

1.2 How Law of Attraction Works: Harmonizing with Nature's Flow

Law of Attraction operates on the principle that our own thoughts and beliefs actively shape the realities we experience. At its core, it asserts that "like attracts like," meaning the energy we project through our thoughts, emotions, and actions draws similar energies of universe. Understanding this concept requires examining the underlying principles, particularly how our mindset impacts the experiences we encounter and the world we create. This process mirrors natural cycles, where factors like sunlight, soil, and water dictate the growth and blossoming of plants. Similarly, our internal landscape of thoughts and beliefs shapes the external reality we perceive.

Central to Law of Attraction is the belief that everything in this universe, including thoughts and emotions, consists of energy. Each thought carries a specific vibrational frequency, akin to a signal sent outward to the universe. When we focus on positive emotions and thoughts, we generate high-frequency energy that attracts favorable experiences and opportunities. Conversely, dwelling on negativity, such as fear or lack, emits lower frequencies, potentially drawing unwanted circumstances. This interplay between internal states and external outcomes parallels how the quality of soil and environment determines a plant's health and vitality.

A critical component of this concept is intention, which acts as a directional force for our thoughts and beliefs. By clearly defining what we are wishing to manifest, we align our energy with our objectives, thereby enhancing focus and facilitating the journey toward our aspirations. Tools like vision boards, affirmations, and meditation reinforce these intentions by embedding them deeply into our subconscious, akin to how roots anchor a tree firmly to the ground, enabling it to flourish.

Beliefs also play a pivotal role in Law of Attraction. Our beliefs influence our perception of the world and our reactions to various situations. Believing in our worthiness for love, success, and abundance makes it easier to attract these elements into our lives. On the other hand, restrictive beliefs, such as feelings of inadequacy or fear of failure, can obstruct our ability to achieve what we desire. Overcoming these barriers involves self-reflection, journaling, or seeking guidance from mentors or professionals who specialize in mindset transformation. This process is analogous to pruning plants to encourage healthier and more robust growth.

Emotions are another significant aspect of Law of Attraction. The universe responds not only to our thoughts but also to the emotions we experience. Positive feelings such as joy, gratitude, and excitement emit higher frequencies, which attract similar uplifting experiences. Negative emotions like anger, resentment, or despair can repel desired outcomes. Cultivating emotional awareness and practicing wellness through mindfulness, gratitude, or letting go of negative feelings helps maintain alignment with our goals. This is similar to a balanced ecosystem, where harmony among elements ensures mutual support and sustenance.

The concept of resonance is often associated to Law of Attraction, suggesting that everything in existence, including people and circumstances, possesses a distinct frequency. By aligning our frequency with that of our aspirations, we attract corresponding opportunities and events. For instance, adopting traits like confidence, determination, and optimism aligns us with an energy of success, much like tuning a channel to capture the desired signal. Just as flowers bloom under optimal seasonal and environmental conditions, individuals thrive when embodying the qualities they seek to attract.

Manifestation extends beyond thoughts or wishes; it necessitates action aligned to our intentions. This involves stepping beyond comfort zones, pursuing new opportunities, networking, and embracing experiences. The universe frequently presents opportunities, but recognizing and seizing them remains our responsibility. This is comparable to how a tree adapts to environmental changes, growing stronger under favorable conditions.

Patience and trust are equally crucial. Frustration often arises when results are not immediate, but the universe operates by its own timeline. Believing that desired outcomes are forthcoming, even when their are not yet visible, is essential for maintaining a positive outlook. During this phase of waiting practicing gratitude and abundance reinforces the belief in our connection to our goals. This approach raises our vibrational frequency and keeps us receptive to unexpected opportunities, much like tending to a garden with faith in its eventual growth.

Surrounding ourselves with positive influences is another vital aspect of Law of Attraction. The people, environments, and media we engage with shape our energy levels. Being around supportive, like-minded individuals creates a nurturing environment that fosters growth and positivity. Similarly, organizing physical spaces to reflect our goals-through decluttering, decoration, or incorporating meaningful symbols-serves as a constant motivator, akin to how balanced natural environments encourage life to thrive.

One prevalent misconception about Law of Attraction is that it advocates passivity. Though positive thinking and visualization are key components, proactive efforts are equally important. Personal growth, continuous learning, and self-improvement play a significant role in manifesting desires. The more we expand our understanding and capabilities, the better equipped we are to achieve our aspirations. Self-reflection is also vital for refining goals and setting effective intentions, much like how nature evolves to adapt and flourish in its surroundings.

Surrendering, another integral concept, does not imply giving up. Instead, it involves releasing the want to control every aspect of how events unfold. It reflects trust in the universe's ability to deliver the best outcomes, even if they diverge from initial expectations. Clinging too tightly for specific results can create resistance, hindering in flow of abundance. Embracing surrender opens up unforeseen possibilities, fostering creativity and flexibility, much like a river naturally finding its course around obstacles.

Lastly, self-love and acceptance form the cornerstone of Law of Attraction. Developing a healthy relationship with oneself lays the foundation for attracting positivity. When we affection and accept ourselves, we radiate confident and joyful energy, making us more receptive to the experiences we seek. Embracing our individuality, celebrating achievements, and giving ourselves by compassion strengthens the belief that we deserve a fulfilling life. This self-assuredness mirrors the resilience of a robust tree, deeply rooted in its surroundings and thriving by drawing strength from within.

1.3 The Science Behind Manifestation: Nature's Blueprint for Creation

Law of Attraction has captivated individuals from various backgrounds, eliciting both curiosity and skepticism. At its essence, Law of Attraction asserts that "like attracts like," emphasizing the power for thoughts and emotions to shape reality we experience. The concept is rooted not only in philosophy and spirituality but also in scientific frameworks involving consciousness, energy, and the universe. To delve deeper into how manifestation functions, it is vital to explore it through the perspectives of psychology, quantum physics, and neuroscience. Much like the natural world, where harmonious interactions among elements foster life, Law of Attraction suggests that our internal energy radiates outward, influencing the external environment we encounter.

A cornerstone of Law of Attraction is the concept of consciousness, envisioned as an expansive ocean of energy. Every thought we generate acts like a pebble dropped into this ocean, creating ripples that impact our surroundings and experiences. Quantum physics provides insights into this phenomenon through the principle of quantum entanglement, which suggests that particles can connect and influence one another across distances. This idea implies that our thoughts, as forms of energy, can interact with the universe in meaningful ways. By focusing on positive outcomes and visualizing our desires, we may align our energy with that of the universe, thereby attracting similar energy back to us- akin to how energy flows through ecosystems, fostering equilibrium and growth.

The observer effect in quantum physics further elucidates this concept, demonstrating that mere observation can alter the behavior of a subject. Applying this principle to human experience suggests that focused attention can shape reality. Concentrating on goals and aspirations allows us to influence outcomes to align with the intentions. This perspective underscores a universal truth: our beliefs and perceptions profoundly affect our experiences, much like sunlight or water influences a plant's development and growth.

From a psychological standpoint, the self-fulfilling prophecy illustrates how expectations can shape reality. Strong belief in one's ability to achieve a goal often leads to actions that bring that goal closer. Conversely, negative thoughts can inadvertently undermine efforts, often without conscious awareness. This highlights the importance of nurturing a positive mindset. By aligning our thoughts with our goals, we establish a mental framework that not only enhances motivation but also attracts opportunities consistent with our intentions. As seeds in fertile soil transform into thriving plants, so too do our thoughts cultivate the reality we nurture.

Neuroscience sheds light on this process through neuroplasticity concept, the brain's capacity to adapt and form new neural connections based on experiences and learning. Consistently focusing on positive thoughts and using affirmations rewires the brain to support these beliefs. Over time, this rewiring fosters a more optimistic outlook, greater resilience, and an increased likelihood of achieving goals. This process creates a reinforcing cycle where positive thoughts lead to positive outcomes, much like rivers gradually sculpting valleys into enduring landscapes.

Emotions are equally critical to manifestation, often described as "energy in motion" that significantly shapes our reality. Aligning emotions with our desires sends a clear signal for universe about our intentions. Positive emotions like joy, gratitude, and love elevate our energy, make it easier to attract favorable experiences. Conversely, negative emotions such as fear or doubt generate denser energy that can obstruct our goals. This demonstrates the importance of emotional awareness and maintaining positivity to enhance manifestation capabilities, akin to how a flourishing forest depends on harmony among its elements.

Practices such as mindfulness and meditation further amplify the effectiveness of Law of Attraction. Mindfulness fosters awareness for thoughts and emotions, enabling individuals to identify and alter negative patterns. Meditation provides a focused space for Visualization along with affirmations, allowing clearer articulation of desired realities. Research shows that regular meditation improves emotional health, reduces stress, and enhances concentration-all of which support more effective manifestation. Much like the stillness of a serene pond reflecting the sky, mindfulness and meditation help align intentions with purposeful action.

Gratitude is another potent tool in manifestation realm. By expressing gratitude, we shift our mindset from scarcity to abundance, raising our vibrational frequency. Acknowledging and appreciating what we already have signals openness to receiving more. This practice fosters a positive cycle where gratitude invites greater abundance. Techniques such as maintaining a gratitude periodical or reflecting on blessings strengthen this connection, nurturing the manifestation process much like rain nourishes the earth, enabling growth and flourishing.

An intriguing aspect of manifestation is the concept of collective consciousness, which suggests a shared reservoir of thoughts, beliefs, and intentions among people. Tapping into this collective energy can amplify personal manifestation efforts. Aligning individual desires with broader, collective goals fosters a powerful synergy that bolsters individual outcomes while cultivating a sense of community and shared purpose. This interconnected energy resembles a grove of trees with intertwined roots, mutually supporting and sustaining one another.

Law of Attraction also emphasizes the significance of intention. Clear and focused intentions provide a guiding framework for realizing aspirations. Regularly refining and revisiting intentions ensures alignment with one's goals, allowing actions to remain on track. Intentions act as a current, much like a river charting its course, steering individuals toward desired destinations while shaping the journey itself.

It is crucial to recognize that manifestation involves more than mere wishing; it requires action. Visualization along with affirmations are vital but must be complemented by tangible efforts. This entails embracing opportunities, stepping beyond comfort zones, and remaining receptive to new experiences. Taking deliberate actions aligned with one's intentions demonstrates commitment to manifesting desired outcomes, inviting universal support. Just as seeds grow when planted in fertile soil and nurtured with care, manifestation flourishes through proactive engagement.

CHAPTER 2

THE POWER OF BELIEF

2.1 The Role of Mindset in Manifestation: Cultivating the Garden of Thought

The mindset we cultivate is vital in process for manifestation process, as it shapes our experiences and determines what we appeal into our lives. The core principle of Law of Attraction suggests, our thoughts and beliefs significantly impact the reality we create. This concept means that whatever we consistently focus on-whether positive or negative-tends to materialize in our lives. Thus, the quality of our mindset profoundly influences how effectively we can apply Law of Attraction. To comprehend this better, we must explore the workings of mindset, its psychological basis, and methods to foster a more positive mental environment for manifestation. Just as a well-tended garden thrives under suitable conditions, our mindset requires nurturing to allow the seeds of manifestation to grow and flourish.

A mindset comprises the beliefs and attitudes we hold about ourselves, others, and the world. These underlying beliefs influence our perceptions and life experiences, often operating subconsciously. For instance, if we view the world as abundant with opportunities, we are likely to recognize and attract them. However, if doubt, negativity, or fear of failure dominates our mindset, we might unconsciously invite limitations and challenges. Cognitive psychology supports this, illustrating how our expectations shape behaviors and outcomes. Similar to how a plant bends toward light, our mindset channels the direction of our energy.

A key distinction within mindset is the contrast between a "fixed" and a "growth" mindset, a concept introduced by psychologist Carol Dweck. A fixed mindset assumes that abilities and intelligence are static, leading to feelings of inadequacy when faced with challenges. Conversely, a growth mindset holds that skills and talents can develop through effort and learning. This perspective promotes resilience and a willingness to take risks-both essential elements of manifestation. Adopting a growth mindset encourages openness to new possibilities and diminishes discouragement the face of obstacles, enabling us to stay optimistic and goal-oriented. Similarly, plants that adapt to their environment, likely to thrive.

Our emotions are deeply intertwined with mindset and significantly influence manifestation. Thoughts directly impact emotions, and emotional states affect our ability for manifest desires. Positive emotions, like gratitude, joy, and love, increase our vibrational frequency, making its easy to attract favorable outcomes. In contrast, negative emotions like fear, anger, or resentment lower this frequency, creating barriers to achieving goals. Managing emotions and aligning thoughts with aspirations is crucial for maintaining a positive mindset, much like ensuring plants receive adequate sunlight and water to prosper.

Visualization serving as a powerful technique for aligning mindset with manifestation objectives. Visualizing our goals is not merely daydreaming but a process of actively engaging the mind and emotions to prepare for success. By vividly picturing our desires, we make them feel tangible and attainable. This clarity helps the mind identify opportunities and paths toward those goals. Many successful individuals credit visualization for creating a strong link between intention and action. Just as gardeners envision a bountiful harvest before planting, we must clearly visualize our objectives to realize them.

Affirmations are another effective tool for shaping mindset. Regularly repeating positive statements about ourselves and our goals helps rewire our thoughts and challenges negative beliefs. Affirmations enhance confidence and foster the belief that we deserve happiness and success. This practice reshapes our self-perception but also transforms our outlook on the world. Consistent use of affirmations gradually shifts our mindset, making it more conducive to manifestation. Like tending a garden regularly, affirmations maintain a fertile mental landscape for growth.

Gratitude plays a vital role in fostering a positive attitude and aiding manifestation. Focusing on gratitude shifts attention from scarcity to abundance, creating a cycle of positivity that enhances our outlook. Expressing gratitude aligns us by energy of abundance, signaling readiness to receive more of universe. This appreciative mindset diminishes feelings of lack or desperation, which can hinder manifestation. Practicing gratitude daily reinforces a mindset that attracts greater positivity, akin to how nourishing soil strengthens plants, enabling them to flourish.

Surrounding oneself with uplifting influences is also important for developing a positive mindset. The people whom we interact with, the media we consume, and the environments we inhabit significantly affect our mental state. Negative influences can drain energy and reinforce limiting beliefs, while positive influences inspire growth and encourage us to persevere. Building connections with compatible individuals creates a supportive environment that enhances manifestation efforts. This collective energy motivates and sustains focus, much like interconnected trees in a forest support one another through their shared root systems.

A resilient mindset requires patience and persistence. The journey toward achieving goals is often unpredictable and fraught with challenges. Maintaining a mindset that embraces resilience and perseverance is crucial during difficult times. Rather than perceiving obstacles as failures, they can be viewed as opportunities for learning and growth. This shift in perspective fosters a focus on long-term objectives instead of succumbing to temporary setbacks. Patience is equally important, as manifestation often unfolds over time. Understanding this helps to prevent frustration and maintain positivity. Just as trees take some time to grow to their full potential, our aspirations require patience and consistent effort to come to fruition.

Self-awareness is another vital aspect of a healthy mindset. Becoming more conscious for thoughts and emotions enables us to identify patterns that may hinder manifestation. With increased awareness, we can challenge negative beliefs and replace them with empowering ones. Practices such as journaling, meditation, and mindfulness enhance self-awareness, providing insights into our mental habits. This intentional focus allows for thoughtful choices that will align with manifestation goals, much like a gardener removing weeds to ensure optimal growth.

Self-care is also integral to sustaining a positive mindset. Taking care of physical, emotional, and mental health directly affects our ability for the manifest desires. Activities such as regular exercise, proper nutrition, and adequate rest help maintain mental clarity and focus. Emotional well-being can be nurtured through meditation, therapy, or creative outlets, allowing us to process emotions and release negative energy that could obstruct manifestation efforts. Prioritizing self-care builds resilience and openness, ensuring the vibrancy of both mind and body. Just like a plant requires care to thrive, our well-being must be nurtured for successful manifestation.

Lastly, recognizing and addressing limiting beliefs is crucial for manifestation. Feelings of unworthiness or inadequacy, often rooted in past experiences or societal conditioning, can create obstacles. Identifying these beliefs and replacing with positive affirmations helps dismantle barriers to success. Techniques like cognitive restructuring, which involves challenging and reformatting negative thoughts, empower individuals to overcome limitations. Much like a plant breaking soil to grow, overcoming to the limiting beliefs allows us to realize our full potential.

2.2 Overcoming to the limiting beliefs: Breaking Through Nature's Barriers to Growth

Overcoming to the limiting beliefs is essential for effectively applying Law of Attractionfor manifest desired outcomes. Limiting beliefs are ingrained convictions that hinder personal growth, often acting as obstacles to pursuing goals and dreams. These beliefs frequently stem from past experiences, societal norms, or internalized negative messages, functioning as barriers to success. Just as stones in the soil obstruct a plant's roots from spreading, limiting beliefs restrict our capability to attract what we truly desire. Clearing these mental obstructions creates fertile ground for manifestation, akin to preparing soil for a thriving garden.

The step first in overcoming to the limiting beliefs is identifying them. This involves introspection and developing self-awareness. It requires examining the narratives we construct about the capabilities, worth, and potential for success. Often, these limiting beliefs operate unconsciously, subtly shaping our decisions and behaviors. For instance, someone raised in an environment where financial scarcity was prevalent may internalize the belief that these are unworthy of financial success. This belief can lead to self-sabotaging actions, such as procrastination or avoiding lucrative opportunities. Recognizing these beliefs is akin to removing rocks and weeds from soil, creating space for new growth.

After identifying limiting beliefs, next step is to challenge them. This process entails questioning the rationality of these beliefs and seeking evidence to refute them. For instance, someone doubting their qualifications for a job can reflect on past achievements and moments of competence. Transitioning from self-doubt to confidence dismantles the barriers created by these negative beliefs. Accepting the origins of limiting beliefs-often rooted in fear or past events rather than factual reality-further aids this transformation. Much like pruning a plant to eliminate dead branches, replacing unhelpful beliefs with healthier perspectives encourages personal growth.

Affirmations is a powerful method for shifting limiting beliefs. Replacing negative thoughts with affirmations allows individuals to reprogram their subconscious minds. Affirmations are concise, positive statements reflecting desired realities. For example, substituting "I am not worthy of success" with "I deserve success and abundance" instills a more empowering narrative. Repeating these affirmations daily gradually transforms thought patterns, fostering self-belief. This practice mirrors the nurturing of seeds, which require time and care to develop into robust plants, symbolizing the patience needed to establish empowering beliefs.

Visualization is another effective strategy for the overcoming of limiting beliefs. By vividly imagining the achievement of goals, individuals create a strong emotional connection to desired outcomes. Visualization helps solidify the belief that aspirations are attainable, aligning personal energy with these objectives. Engaging all senses during visualization enhances its impact, evoking the emotions of success as though it has already occurred. This emotional resonance elevates one's vibrational frequency, drawing desires closer to reality. Visualization is akin to envisioning a blooming flower, laying the groundwork for success before it materializes.

Surrounding oneself with positive influences is also crucial for addressing limiting beliefs. The environments and people we engage with can either reinforce or dismantle these beliefs. Building connections with supportive friends, mentors, or communities fosters encouragement and growth. Learning from individuals who have overcome their own limiting beliefs provides both inspiration and actionable strategies. Their success stories affirm that transformation is possible. Just as trees in a forest support one another through interconnected roots, a supportive network reinforces personal growth and resilience.

Reframing failure is another key to overcoming to the limiting beliefs. Many such beliefs originate from the fear of failure and its perceived judgment. By viewing failure as an opportunity for learning rather than a reflection of worth, its intimidating power diminishes. Each setback provides lessons that strengthen resilience and adaptability. Changing one's perspective on failure weakens the influence of restrictive beliefs, fostering a mindset that embraces challenges. Much like plants bending toward sunlight despite obstacles, individuals can learn to thrive by adapting to adversity.

Mindfulness and meditation further assist in overcoming to the limiting beliefs. These practices promote awareness for thoughts and emotions, enabling individuals to recognize negative patterns without judgment. Mindfulness fosters present-moment awareness, helping individuals identify and replace limiting beliefs with empowering thoughts. Meditation creates a focused space for self-reflection and mental clarity. Observing thought patterns, much like noticing seasonal changes in nature, allows individuals to make adjustments that support growth and alignment with their goals.

Adopting a growing mindset is transformative in challenging limiting beliefs. A growth mindset embraces the potential for improvement through effort and learning, viewing obstacles as opportunities rather than insurmountable barriers. This perspective inspires resilience, risk-taking, and confidence, essential qualities for manifestation. Much like plants reaching for sunlight, a growth mindset propels individuals toward achieving their fullest potential.

Journaling is a treasured tool for addressing limiting beliefs. Writing down thoughts and emotions provides insights into patterns and beliefs that hinder progress. Journaling offers a platform to explore the roots of these beliefs and rewrite them into empowering narratives. Tracking progress through journaling fosters motivation and highlights personal growth. Like tending a garden, journaling nurtures mental and emotional well-being, ensuring a mindset conducive to manifestation.

Continuous learning and self-improvement play a key and essential role in overcoming to the limiting beliefs. Expanding knowledge and skills bolsters confidence and equips individuals to challenge negative patterns of thoughts. Engaging in educational activities aligned with personal goals signals readiness to embrace desired outcomes. This commitment to growth mirrors the steady strengthening of a tree, which becomes more resilient and expansive with timely care.

Accountability is another effective strategy for breaking free from limiting beliefs. Sharing goals with a trusted friend, coach, or mentor provides external support and motivation. An accountability partner offers encouragement, constructive feedback, and guidance, helping maintain focus and momentum. This support acts as a stabilizing force, much like a trellis supports a climbing plant, enabling growth in alignment with one's intentions.

2.3 Cultivating a Growth Mindset: Nurturing the Garden of Personal

Growth

Cultivating for growth mindset is fundamental for effectively leveraging Law of Attraction to manifest your aspirations. A growing mindset likened to a vibrant garden, thriving and evolving through consistent effort, learning, and persistence. This perspective is rooted in the belief of abilities and intelligence can expand and improve, much like a plant that strengthens and flourishes with proper care and nourishment. In sharp contrast, a fixed mindset holds that traits are immutable, similar to a plant confined to poor soil. Embracing a growing mindset fosters resilience, adaptability, and the belief in the capacity to create the life you desire-key factors in manifestation, just as a healthy plant draws strength from its surroundings to reach its full potential.

Psychologist Carol Dweck introduced the growth mindset concept through her research on learning and achievement. She demonstrated that individuals with a growing mindset embrace challenges, that persist through obstacles, and view failure as a chance to learn rather than as a limitation. This mindset can be compared to a tree that bends but does not break in the wind, becoming stronger with every storm. Within the framework of Law of Attraction, adopting this mindset helps align the thoughts and beliefs with your goals, much like how plants instinctively turn toward sunlight to thrive.

A significant transformation occurs when developing for growth mindset: a shift in how challenges are perceived. Instead of shying away from difficulties, you begin to face them with curiosity and a inclination to grow. This outlook is essential for manifestation. According to Law of Attraction, the energy you emit-whether positive or negative-is reflected back to you. Viewing challenges as insurmountable creates frustration and negativity, while seeing them as opportunities raises your vibrational energy and attracts positive outcomes. Similar to a plant that adapts to its environment for survival, this proactive mindset keeps you focused on your objectives and reinforces the belief in your ability to achieve them.

Resilience is another vital component for growth mindset, essential for navigating the manifestation process. Life's unpredictability often disrupts plans, but with a growing mindset, setbacks become part for learning curve rather than signs of failure. This resilience enables you to remain positive and focused, even when faced with long adversity. Instead of abandoning your aspirations, you can adjust strategies and continue moving forward, staying aligned with your intentions. This flexibility complements Law of Attraction, which emphasizes maintaining for a good outlook and faith in your goals to bring them closer to fruition. Like plants that sway with the wind but remain firmly rooted, resilience grounds you during life's challenges.

Openness to feedback and learning from others is another hallmark for growth mindset. While independence is valuable, seeking advice and guidance can improve your ability to manifest your desires. Constructive feedback allows you to refine your skills and explore new approaches to attaining your goals. Surrounding yourself with supportive, growth-oriented individuals also amplifies your success. Law of Attraction thrives on positive connections, and engaging with like-minded people creates a productive environment for your manifestations to flourish. This collective energy is akin to planting yourself in nutrient-rich soil, where shared encouragement strengthens your intentions.

Curiosity and a passion for learning are also key to fostering a growth mindset. Embracing a love of learning unlocks doors to new experiences that support personal growth and align with your goals. When you remain curious, you are recognize and seize opportunities presented by the universe. Law of Attraction emphasizes the importance of being ready to act on these opportunities, and a growth mindset keeps you attuned to the possibilities around you. Much like how plants continuously adapt to seasonal changes, a growth mindset allows you to grow and evolve with your environment.

The language you use significantly influences your mindset. Individuals of growth mindset adopt language that reflects optimism and the potential for improvement. Phrases such as "I can grow from this experience" or "I'm capable of learning" reinforce the belief in self-development. In contrast, negative self-talk fuels a fixed mindset, fostering doubt and limiting beliefs. By choosing words that empower and uplift, to align your thoughts and energy with the outcomes you desire. This creates a cycle where positive thoughts drive positive actions, leading to positive results-much like the natural cycle of growth in a thriving ecosystem.

CHAPTER 3

SETTING INTENTIONS

3.1 The Importance of Setting Clear Intentions: Navigating Life with Nature's Compass

Establishing clear intentions is a foundational aspect of utilizing Law of Attraction to manifest your aspirations. Intentions act as a guiding compass, steering your thoughts, emotions, and actions toward your desired outcomes. Much like how nature's cycles adhere to specific patterns, setting well-defined intentions allows you to shape your reality with purpose. This process extends beyond mere hope, demanding clarity, focus, and a deep understanding of what you truly seek-akin to planting seeds deliberately to ensure they grow into healthy, thriving plants.

The importance of clear intentions denigrations in their ability to ignite the manifestation process. Intentions transform vague wishes into precise, actionable goals, similar to how sunlight directs a plant's growth. The universe responds most effectively to specific and focused signals. Ambiguous or scattered intentions make it challenging for circumstances to align in your favor. For instance, rather than setting a general intention to "be happy," a more precise goal might be "to find joy through creative expression." This specificity sharpens your focus and increases the likelihood of taking meaningful steps toward your goal, just as nature flourishes when provided with clear and nurturing conditions.

Emotions drama a pivotal role in amplifying the power of intentions. They act as potent amplifiers, much like the wind dispersing seeds across a landscape. Associating positive emotions with your intentions increases your vibrational frequency, attracting corresponding positive energies of universe. For example, like intention is to secure a new job, visualizing not just the position but also the associated feelings of excitement, gratitude, and satisfaction can greatly enhance the manifestation process. These emotions fuel your motivation to act, reinforcing your intention and drawing opportunities closer to you, much like a tree reaching for sunlight as its source of nourishment.

Authenticity is crucial when setting intentions. Many individuals unknowingly set goals based on societal expectations or external pressures rather than their true desires. Pursuing inauthentic intentions can result in dissatisfaction or unfulfilled aspirations. To prevent this, dedicate time to self-reflection, identifying what genuinely matters to you and aligns with your values and passions. By grounding your intentions in authenticity, the manifestation process becomes more meaningful and rewarding. Just as a river naturally follows its true course, your intentions must flow from your core to reach their ultimate destination.

Visualization is an invaluable tool for clarifying intentions. Creating vivid mental images for desired outcomes engages your subconscious mind, similar to how a gardener envisions a flourishing harvest before planting. Visualization strengthens the belief in achieving your goals, enhancing your ability to recognize opportunities that support them. As you visualize success, you begin noticing signs, people, and circumstances that will align with your vision, making it easier for whole universe to assist you. Visualization is like watching a flower bloom in your mind, preparing the soil for success and encouraging it to come to life.

Clear intentions also provide guidance for decision-making and action. When confronted with choices, referring to your intentions helps determine the most aligned path. This focus prevents distractions, much like how plants grow toward sunlight. For instance, if you've set an intention to adopt a healthier lifestyle, you will likely to choose nutritious meals and regular exercise over habits that conflict with your goal. Intentions not only clarify your desires but also inspire consistent actions toward achieving them, akin to how plants continuously grow toward their source of nourishment.

Recognizing that intentions will lead to immediate results is essential. The universe operates in the own timeline, similar to the natural progression of seasons. Patience is key for manifestation process. Trusting that will desires are on their way-even if not immediately visible-maintains a positive mindset. This trust keeps you open to opportunities along synchronicities that help fulfill your intentions in due time, much like a seed requiring time to grow into a flourishing tree.

Flexibility is another important aspect of setting intentions. As you evolve, your desires can shift, much like a river altering its course over time. Regularly revisiting and adjusting your intentions ensures they remain aligned with your current aspirations and circumstances. This adaptability prevents frustration when things do not unfold as originally expected. By remaining open to change, you maintain a sense of flow in your manifestation journey, much like nature's resilience in adapting to shifting environments.

Accountability plays a supportive role in the intention-setting process. Sharing your intentions with trusted friends, mentors, or a community offers encouragement and keeps you committed. This external support system is particularly valuable when encountering self-doubt or challenges. Collaborating with individuals who share alike goals provides fresh perspectives and bolsters motivation. Just as plants in an ecosystem thrive through shared resources, connecting with others strengthens your journey by amplifying collective energy.

Incorporating rituals or practices into your intention-setting routine reinforces your commitment. Writing intentions in a journal, creating vision boards, or using meditation to focus on goals adds a purpose sense to the process. These rituals serve as daily reminders of your aspirations, keeping you motivated and enthusiastic, much like the daily sunlight that nourishes plant growth.

3.2 How to Set Effective Goals: Planting Seeds for Growth and Success

Setting effective goals is a vital step in using Law of Attraction to manifest your desires. Goals serve as seeds planted in the fertile ground of your mind, directing your energy, thoughts, and actions toward realizing your aspirations. Manifestation is not merely about wishing for something; it involves creating clear, actionable steps that align the mindset with your desired outcomes. The clarity and structure of your goals significantly influence how successfully you can manifest them, much like seeds require are right conditions to grow, as the universe responds to your energy and focus.

The step first in goal setting is ensuring specificity. Vague goals can lead to vague results, while clear and detailed goals provide the universe with focused signals, much like seeds requiring particular nutrients, water, and sunlight to thrive. For example, instead of stating, "I want to be successful," specify, "I want to start a business within a year that generates $5,000 monthly." This level of precision offers a clear target, making visualization more vivid and attainable. A specific goal creates a mental image akin to a well-planned garden flourishing under intentional care.

Measurability is another key component of effective goals. Goals that can be measured allow to track progress and celebrate achievements along the way. For instance, like to the broad aim of "getting healthier," a measurable goal might be "losing 15 pounds in three months." Breaking goals into measurable parts provides a clear pathway, reinforcing confidence as milestones are reached. Monitoring your progress, much like a farmer observing crop growth, ensures your efforts align with desired outcomes and keep you motivated.

Goals must also be attainable. While dreaming big is important, setting unrealistic goals lead to discouragement. Balance ambition with practicality by considering the resources, skills, and time available. For example, instead of aiming to write a bestseller in one month, set a realistic goal such as completing the first draft of a book within six months. Achievable goals foster steady progress, much like how a tree grows gradually and solidly over time rather than shooting up overnight.

Aligning goals with your values and passions ensures long-term commitment and excitement. Reflect on what truthfully matters to you-whether career growth, relationships, health, or financial stability. Goals that reverberate with your core values are more likely to sustain your focus and energy. For instance, financial goals aligned with values of security and generosity are more compelling, keeping you motivated to achieve them. Just as a tree's roots must be grounded in nourishing soil, your goals should be rooted in what genuinely fulfills you.

Setting a timeframe for your goals enhances their effectiveness. Deadlines create urgency and structure, encouraging action and helping you visit on track. For example, like goal is to complete a marathon within a year, set monthly milestones to build endurance gradually. Timeframes help guide your efforts, allowing adjustments as needed while ensuring steady progress. Similar to how seasons dictate the growth of plants, a timeline directs your journey toward achieving your objectives.

Visualization is the powerful technique for goal achievement. Taking time to imagine yourself reaching your goal engages your subconscious mind, reinforcing belief in its attainability. Find a quiet place and vividly picture what success looks and feels like. Engage your senses-what do you can see, hear, and feel in that moment? This immersive visualization strengthens your intention, making the desired outcome feel real. The clearer your vision, the more effectively you can attract it, much like a seed's unobstructed path to sunlight enables it to grow.

Affirmations further support goal realization. Repeating positive statements about your goals helps train with the subconscious mind to believe in the ability to succeed. For example, if career advancement is your aim, affirmations like, "I am confident and capable of achieving success in my career," align your thoughts with the intentions. These affirmations act as nourishment, feeding your mindset and strengthening your belief, much like water sustains a plant's growth.

Maintaining positive attitude is crucial throughout the goal-setting process. Positivity fosters resilience, allowing you to view the challenges for opportunities rather than setbacks. An optimistic mindset aligns with growth principles mindset, keeping you open to unexpected solutions and opportunities presented by the universe. Much like how nature adapts and thrives under changing conditions, a positive outlook enables you to adjust and grow in goals pursuit.

Accountability is another essential element of effective goal setting. Sharing your intentions with a trusted mentor, friend, or community creating a sense of responsibility and motivation. Having a support system provides encouragement, feedback, and helps you stay focused. Whether through a mentor or a group sharing similar aspirations, external accountability strengthens your commitment. Just as plants thrive within supportive ecosystems, you benefit from a network that nurtures your progress.

Flexibility is also vital when pursuing goals. Life's unpredictability can require you to reassess and adjust your plans. Being adaptable allows you to navigate setbacks and explore new opportunities, without losing vision of your larger aspirations. Flexibility doesn't mean forsaking; it means flowing with change and discovering alternative paths to success. Much like a river that adjusts its course around obstacles, flexibility enables you to maintain momentum toward your ultimate goal.

3.3 Aligning Intentions with Your Values: Rooting Your Desires in Nature's Truth

Setting intentions is a precarious component of the manifestation process, serving as a framework to focus your thoughts, emotions, and actions on achieving your goals. Aligning these intentions with your values is vital to ensure that what you aim to attract is deeply connected to your authentic self. This alignment is comparable to planting seeds in fertile soil, creating a foundation that allows your desires to take root and flourish. It enhances the effectiveness of manifestation but also ensures the journey is meaningful and fulfilling, much like how nature prospers when in harmony with its environment.

Values are the superintendent principles that shape your decisions and behaviors, forming the foundation of your life much like the roots of a tree. When your intentions align for values, they become more than just goals-they transform into affirmations of your identity and purpose. This connection ensures that with thoughts, emotions, and actions resonate with for true self. Setting intentions that reflect your values channels your energy authentically, much like how plants naturally grow toward sunlight, making it easier to attract what you genuinely desire.

The step first in aligning your intentions with your values is clarifying what those values are. Dedicate time to self-reflection by asking questions such as: What do I stand for? What brings me happiness? What impact do I want to make? These reflections may span areas like relationships, career, personal growth, health, and spirituality. Writing your values down can solidify your understanding and serve as a reference when setting intentions. This process is akin to a gardener assessing the soil before planting, ensuring the best conditions for growth.

Once your values are clear, the very next-step is crafting intentions that reflect them. Intentions should be specific, positive, and framed in a present tense. For example, rather than saying, "I want to be successful," you could express, "I am attracting opportunities to express my creativity and make a positive impact." This phrasing not only aligns with a value of creativity but also focuses on contribution. Such clarity helps form a intense mental image of your desired reality, making it easier for your subconscious to guide your actions. Just as nature thrives in balance, your intentions gain strength when grounded in your core values.

It's imperative to recognize that values can evolve over time. Life experiences, personal development, and changing circumstances can shift your priorities. Regularly reassessing your values and intentions helps maintain their relevance and keeps you connected with inner self. Journaling can be a valuable tool for this reflection, offering a space to explore thoughts, track changes, and deepen self-awareness. Much like how nature adjusts to seasonal changes, revisiting and adapting your intentions ensures they remain aligned with your current values.

Aligning intentions with values also infuses authenticity into the manifestation process. When your desires align with your true self, you naturally exude confidence and conviction, attracting opportunities and people who resonate with your energy. Conversely, intentions that conflict with your values may lead to dissatisfaction, even if the goals are achieved. This misalignment can generate a sense of emptiness, similar to a plant struggling to grow in inadequate soil. Authentic alignment ensures that both the journey and the outcome are fulfilling.

Emotional resonance is another critical element in aligning intentions with values. When your intentions reflect your values, you likely to experience positive emotions throughout the process. Emotions are central to Law of Attraction-positive feelings raise your vibrational frequency, drawing similar energies. Pursuing goals misaligned with your values can generate frustration or anxiety, lowering your vibration and hindering manifestation. Ensuring your intentions match your values enhances both your ability for manifest and your overall sense of well-being, much like how a well-tended plant grows strong and vibrant.

This alignment also fosters a strong sense of purpose. Goals that reflect your values often feel more meaningful, motivating you to persevere through challenges. Your values serve as a compass, guiding your decisions and helping you evaluate opportunities based on how well they align with your intentions. This clarity empowers for to take purposeful actions that lead to both your desired outcomes and personal fulfillment, much like trees growing stronger when deeply rooted in nourishing soil.

CHAPTER 4

VISUALIZATION TECHNIQUES

4.1 The Visualization power in Manifestation: Nurturing the Seeds of Your Dreams

Visualization is the powerful technique central to Law of Attraction and the manifestation process. It involves crafting detailed and bright mental images of the outcomes or experiences you wish to bring into your life. Unlike casual daydreaming, visualization is an intentional practice that combines focus, emotional engagement, and a strong understanding of your desires. It acts like nurturing seeds planted in fertile soil, helping them grow into tangible reality. By aligning with subconscious mind and conscious goals, visualization bridges the gap between your present state and the future you aspire to create.

Psychologically, visualization is effective because the brain cannot differentiate between real and vividly imagined experiences. When you visualize, the brain triggers neural pathways as if you were living the event, a phenomenon called "mental rehearsal." This principle is commonly used by athletes who visualize flawless performances to enhance their actual abilities. The same process can be applied to manifesting personal goals, whether they involve career advancement, relationships, or self-improvement. Like a gardener envisioning a thriving harvest, visualization allows you to plant for seeds of your aspirations in your mind, nurturing them into fruition.

The step first to effective visualization is developing a clear and specific vision of your goals. Ambiguous desires dilute the visualization power, much like scattering seeds carelessly leads to uneven growth. Instead of imagining generic success, focus on what success specifically means to you-whether it's a particular job, lifestyle, or personal achievement. This clarity provides your mind with a precise target, enhancing visualization's impact, much like planting a seed in optimal conditions increases its chances of thriving.

Incorporating all your senses during visualization is essential for creating a more immersive experience. By engage your senses, you make your visualization feel more tangible. Picture what you see, but also imagine the associated sounds, textures, scents, and even tastes. For instance, if visualizing career success, you might imagine the feel of your desk, the aroma of coffee, the sound of supportive conversations, and the sight of a workspace that inspires you. This multi-sensory approach strengthens the emotional and psychological impact of your visualization, much like how nature's elements work together to foster the growth of a robust plant.

Emotional engagement is a acute component of effective visualization. The emotions you associate with your visualization act as powerful amplifiers, enhancing your connection to your desires. While visualizing, immerse in the feelings you would experience like goals were already achieved-whether it's joy, gratitude, peace, or excitement. These emotions signal your subconscious mind that your envisioned reality is attainable, reinforcing belief in its manifestation. Like sunlight and water nourishing a seed, emotional engagement provides the energy your intentions need to grow.

To maximize the benefits of visualization, key is consistency. Set aside time every day to practice visualization, integrating it into your routine. Whether in the morning, during a break, or before bed, regular practice ensures that your goals remain at the lead of your mind. Just as a plant needs consistent sunlight and water, daily visualization nurtures your aspirations, keeping them alive and thriving.

Creating the right environment enhances the effectiveness of visualization. Choose a quiet and comfortable space free from distractions. You might dim the lights, play calming music, or introduce soothing scents to foster a peaceful atmosphere. Tools like vision boards, guided meditations, or journals can also help you focus and clarify your visualizations. Similar to how a plant flourishes in a supportive environment, your visualizations gain strength in a setting that encourages focus and clarity.

Belief plays a essential role in the success of visualization. Your beliefs about what is possible greatly influence the effectiveness of your practice. Doubts or resistance can undermine your efforts, so cultivating a positive mindset is essential. Repeating affirmations such as, "I am capable of achieving my dreams," or, "I attract success effortlessly," during your visualization sessions can help overcome limiting beliefs. This practice clears mental blocks, much like removing weeds to allow a garden to flourish.

Visualization is not a passive exercise-it must paired with action. While visualizing aligns your energy for goals, taking inspired steps toward your aspirations ensures their realization. This might involve setting actionable goals, pursuing new opportunities, or simply staying open to possibilities. Think of visualization as the spark that drives toward purposeful actions, much like how internal energy and external conditions work together to enable growth in nature.

Mindfulness can deepen your visualization practice. Before beginning, take a few moments to ground yourself and cultivate a present-focused state of mind. Mindfulness allows you to approach visualization with clarity and intention, enhancing your ability to connect with your goals. By observing your thoughts and emotions without judgment, you create a calm mental environment that supports effective visualization. Similar to a tranquil river reflecting its surroundings, mindfulness sets the stage for visualizations to flow naturally.

4.2 Creating a Vision Board: Mapping Your Path to Manifestation with Nature's Guidance

Creating a vision board is an impactful visualization method that provides a tangible reflection of your dreams and aspirations. It acts as a consistent prompt of what you hope to accomplish, channeling your thoughts and energy toward manifesting those desires. Anchored in the principles of Law of Attraction, vision boards operate on the belief that concentrated focus expands possibilities, much like well-nurtured seeds blossoming into thriving plants. By assembling images, words, or symbols that vibrate with your goals, you craft a visual picture of your aspirations-similar to designing a garden of dreams that requires attention and care to flourish.

The step first in building a vision board involves clearly identifying what you wish to manifest in life. These aspirations can span areas such as self-improvement, career advancement, relationships, health, or financial security. Reflecting on your true desires is essential, akin to a gardener thoughtfully selecting seeds that are compatible with the soil. Clarity in your goals ensures a focused projection of your energy. Instead of vague intentions such as "I want to be happy," opt for a more defined objective, such as "I want to achieve inner peace and joy through regular meditation and spending quality time with family." Specific, detailed goals enhance the effectiveness of your vision board in guiding your manifestation journey, much like choosing the right seeds leads to a lush, vibrant garden.

Once your goals are clearly outlined, the next step is to gather materials for your vision board. Depending on your preference, you can use physical items like poster boards, corkboards, or opt for digital formats using apps or online tools. For physical boards, collect magazines, printed photos, quotes, and other items that align with aspirations. Supplies like scissors, glue, markers, and decorative elements such as stickers or washi tape allow for personalization. Digital platforms like Pinterest or Canva offer flexibility and easy updates for creating a virtual board. Just as different plants require specific tools and care, your vision sheet should reflect your unique objectives and evolve alongside your growth.

With materials ready, the creative process of selecting images and words begins. This step resembles designing a garden filled with meaningful flowers, plants, and decorative features. Look for visuals that embody the experiences and achievements you aim to manifest. Whether it's pictures of dream destinations, symbols of success, or figures of inspiration, these images should evoke strong emotions of enthusiasm and possibility. Including motivational quotes and affirmations strengthens the mindset essential to pursue your dreams. The chosen visuals should create an emotional connection, akin to planting seeds in fertile soil with the expectation that they will bloom into your envisioned reality.

As you assemble your board, consider its layout and design. There are no strict rules for constructing a vision board-it should reflect your individuality and aspirations, much like every garden has its own unique design. Some prefer a neatly categorized board, while others enjoy a more organic, eclectic arrangement. The process of arranging the board can be meditative, fostering a deeper connection with your goals. Visualize what each element represents as you place it, imagining the life you will lead once that aspiration is realized. This act of visualization strengthens your bond with your desires, enhancing the manifestation process-just as imagining a garden in full bloom guides its creation.

Once completed, position your vision board location where you will see it often, such as your bedroom, workspace, or another frequented area. This ensures that vision and goals remain front and center in daily life, much like a well-placed plant receives consistent sunlight for growth. Regularly viewing your board reinforces your dedication to your objectives and aligns your energy with what you seek to manifest. It acts as a visual anchor, maintaining a positive and focused mindset amidst daily distractions, similar to how gardeners diligently tend to their plants.

To boost the impression of your vision board, integrate daily practices that align with goals. Dedicate moments each day to envisaging dreams as though they have already can come true. Incorporate this into your morning routine or as a reflective exercise before bed. During these visualizations, engage all your senses-imagine what you can see, hear, and feel once your goals are achieved. Immersing yourself in these emotions reinforces your belief is attainability of your aspirations, much like watering and nurturing a plant ensures its steady development.

Sharing your dream board with supportive friends or family can amplify its influence. Expressing your goals to others invites accountability and encouragement, fostering an environment of support. This act of sharing can exposed pathways to new opportunities, insights, and connections, enriching your manifestation journey. Discussing your vision with others container also inspire them to pursue their dreams, creating a collective atmosphere of positivity and ambition. This communal energy resembles an ecosystem where diverse elements contribute to mutual growth and success..

4.3 Guided Visualization Exercises: Harnessing Nature's Energy for Manifestation

Guided visualization exercises are highly effective tools for leveraging Law of Attraction and facilitating manifestation. They offer a structured approach that permits individuals to connect deeply with their aspirations, harmonizing their thoughts, emotions, and energy with their desired outcomes. Much like a seed drawing nourishment from the earth, sunlight, and water to produce into a robust plant, guided visualization crystallizes one's intentions, creating an emotional connection that attracts those goals into reality.

At the heart of guided visualization is the use for mental imagery. Participants typically find a calm, distraction-free space, akin to how nature thrives in serene environments. By closing their eyes and imagining their goals, individuals engage all their senses-visualizing the scene, hearing associated sounds, feeling textures, and even invoking smells or tastes. This sensory immersion enhances the vividness of the visualization, encouraging the brain to interpret it as real. Much like a tree grounding itself in fertile soil, this mind-body connection deepens emotional resonance, amplifying the visualization's effectiveness in process for manifestation process.

A common approach to guided visualization involves recorded sessions or scripts that lead participants through the exercise. These guides often begin with grounding techniques to help individuals relax and eliminate distractions, mirroring the calm of a still forest before growth occurs. Once centered, the guide introduces a scenario tied to the participant's goals. For example, someone wishing to manifest a novel career might visualize confidently stepping into their dream workplace, feeling a profound sense of accomplishment and joy. The guide may emphasize vivid details, such as the hum of conversations, the warmth of the environment, and the satisfaction of meaningful work. This detailed imagery reinforces belief, much like envisioning a plant's journey from seed to bloom strengthens its reality.

Another variation of guided visualization integrates affirmations, which are positive announcements that will reinforce a desired belief or reality. Combining affirmations with visualization creates a potent synergy. For instance, during a session focused on career advancement, a participant might repeat affirmations like, "I am deserving of my ideal job," or "Opportunities flow to me with ease." Repeating these affirmations within the visualization reinforces the participant's confidence and mindset, much like nature's cyclical processes that consistently support growth and renewal.

Consistency is essential for guided visualization to yield results. Like any skill, regular practice strengthens its impact, much like plants thrive under consistent sunlight and water. Practicing visualization daily or several times a week deepens the participant's connection to their goals, training the mind to accept these aspirations as attainable. Over time, the brain begins to treat the visualized scenarios as potential realities, gradually shifting energy and attitude to align for desired outcomes. This steady practice mirrors the gradual and deliberate process of growth in nature, fostering trust and patience in the manifestation journey.

Pairing meditation with guided visualization can further enhance its benefits. Meditation, akin to the stillness of a tranquil pond, clears the mind, sharpens focus, and heightens awareness of one's thoughts and emotions. Spending a few moments meditating before visualization helps individuals release distractions, enabling them to engage more fully in the process. This fusion of mindfulness and visualization creates a powerful sense of presence, much like a tree naturally aligning with sunlight for optimal growth.

To personalize guided visualization, incorporating symbols, people, or places with personal significance can intensify its effectiveness. For instance, someone seeking better health might visualize themselves vibrant and energized, surrounded by the beauty of nature-a scene that mirrors the vitality of a thriving ecosystem. Choosing imagery that holds deep personal meaning strengthens emotional resonance, much like rich soil nourishing seeds to foster robust growth.

Guided visualization can also target specific areas for life, like relationships, finances, or personal growth. For relationships, participants might visualize feelings of love, connection, and joy in meaningful interactions. This could include shared experiences or heartfelt conversations, fostering the energy wanted to attract fulfilling relationships. For financial goals, visualizing abundance might involve picturing financial stability, making significant purchases, or enjoying the peace of financial freedom. These mental rehearsals align energy with abundance, much like a steady river flowing toward its destination.

In personal growth, guided visualization can be transformative. Imagining oneself overcoming obstacles or embodying desired traits such as confidence, creativity, or resilience can lead to profound behavioral shifts. For instance, someone working to improve public speaking might visualize delivering a powerful speech to an appreciative audience, evoking feelings of pride and success. This process builds confidence and aligns energy with the desired reality, much like a tree growing stronger after weathering storms.

Guided visualization is an active practice that requires engagement and belief for potential for success. Doubts and fears may arise, but admitting and addressing these emotions helps clear mental blocks that could hinder progress. Journaling or reflecting on these feelings before or after visualization offers clarity and aids in releasing limiting beliefs, much like clearing a garden of obstacles to allow plants to thrive.

CHAPTER 5

THE POWER OF GRATITUDE

5.1 How Gratitude Enhances Manifestation: Embracing Nature's Abundance

Gratitude is widely recognized as one of the most transformative emotional states, especially within the context of Law of Attraction and manifestation. It extends beyond simply expressing thanks for favorable circumstances, encompassing a profound acknowledgment of the abundance and positivity already present in one's life. This recognition is akin to appreciating the natural beauty and resources for world around us, creating a magnetic energy field that aligns with frequencies of abundance, which are fundamental for successful manifestation. The interconnected nature for thoughts/emotions mirrors the systems in nature, where harmony fosters growth. According to Law of Attraction, like attracts like, so cultivating high-vibrational emotions such as gratitude draws in experiences that resonate with those frequencies, much like flowers attract bees to sustain life.

A primary benefit of gratitude is its ability to redirect focus from what is lacking to what is already present, similar to valuing a thriving forest before planting new trees. This shift in perspective fosters a mindset of abundance rather than scarcity, which is vital for manifestation. By concentrating on existing blessings, individuals nurture an appreciation of present, creating emotional balance and aligning their energetic frequency with that of the universe. This mindset strengthens emotional well-being and encourages openness to greater blessings, much like sunlight guiding a plant's growth, signaling readiness to receive more.

Gratitude is also intrinsically linked to positive emotions, which are integral to the manifestation process. Research in psychology demonstrates that positive emotions broaden one's perspective and enhance creativity, akin to how biodiversity strengthens ecosystems. Visualization is a cornerstone of the manifestation, becomes more vivid and impactful when imbued with gratitude. When grateful, visualizations are infused with emotional energy, making them more compelling and aligned with desired outcomes. This emotional charge propels individuals toward their goals, much like a river effortlessly flows toward the sea, carrying momentum and clarity.

Moreover, gratitude fosters resilience, an essential quality for navigating the challenges that often accompany the manifestation journey. Just as trees flex and endure strong winds without breaking, gratitude enables individuals to reframe setbacks as opportunities for growth. Challenges are no longer perceived as failures but as valuable lessons that promote evolution. This perspective shift helps maintain placement with one's intentions, ensuring positive energy and focus. Resilience, much like nature's capacity to adapt, is a cornerstone of maintaining the momentum necessary for manifesting desires.

Incorporating gratitude into daily life can be achieved through practices such as maintaining a gratitude journal. Writing down things for which one is thankful serves as planting seeds of positivity that grow into a flourishing mindset of appreciation. Revisiting these entries provides an chance to reflect on progress and recognize manifestations already achieved. This practice fosters a cycle of positive reinforcement, strengthening the manifestation process, much like how a well-tended plant thrives across seasons. Expressing gratitude toward others further enriches relationships and creates a supportive environment, akin to plants in an ecosystem mutually supporting each other's growth.

Another effective way to amplify manifestation through gratitude is by incorporating it into affirmations. Affirmations is a positive statements that affirm desired outcomes, and pairing them with gratitude intensifies their impact. For instance, instead of saying, "I am wealthy," a more powerful affirmation would be, "I am grateful for the abundance flowing into my life." This slight adjustment adds an emotional dimension, much like how fertile soil enriches seeds, making the affirmation resonate more deeply with the universe. Gratitude enhances the energy behind the words, increasing their potency, similar to how sunlight nurtures a plant's growth.

Gratitude also plays an essential role in aligning with the timing of manifestation. Just as seeds require time to sprout, desires may take time to materialize. Cultivating gratitude for individually step of the journey helps alleviate frustration, fostering patience and acceptance. Appreciating small victories laterally the way creates peace and opens pathways for synchronicities and opportunities to unfold, much like the natural cycles of seasons guide the growth of plants. This mindset encourages trust for universe's timing, allowing manifestations to occur in unexpected yet perfect ways.

Physiologically, gratitude has been shown for reduced stress and promote overall well-being, both of which are critical for effective manifestation. Lower stress levels improve focus and enable individuals to take inspired action toward their goals. This harmony among mind, body, and spirit creates an optimal environment for manifestation, similar to how a balanced ecosystem promotes growth. Additionally, when individuals feel good emotionally and physically, they emit positive liveliness that attracts like-minded people and opportunities, amplifying their manifestation efforts.

Gratitude creates a self-reinforcing feedback loop of positivity, much like rain nourishing the land to support new growth. The more gratitude is practiced, the more reasons one finds to feel grateful. This cycle of gratitude strengthens high-vibrational states, attracting even more positive experiences. The universe responds to the energy one emits, and consistent gratitude elevates vibrational frequencies, enhancing the ability of manifest desires, much like a thriving ecosystem drawing in life and vitality.

5.2 Daily Gratitude Practices: Cultivating the Seeds of Manifestation

Gratitude is a transformative force that enhances emotional well-being while aligning with the universal energies that drive manifestation. Regularly practicing gratitude fosters an energetic exchange with the universe, much like the cyclical patterns in nature that sustain balance and abundance. By appreciating what we already had, we attune ourselves to the rhythms that govern life, creating a flow of positivity that attracts more we desire. Daily gratitude practices deepen this connection, fostering a mindset that nurtures manifestation, similar to how a well-tended garden flourishes over time.

One of the most impactful ways to include gratitude into daily life is by maintaining a gratitude journal. This practice mirrors nature's cycles, where every season introduces new phases of growth. By documenting three things you're grateful for each day, you create a continuous exchange of positive energy with the world. This reflective process, much like a seed's germination, cultivates appreciation and enriches the mental soil necessary for manifestations to take root. Consistently engaging for practice broadens awareness of life's abundance, akin to ecosystems thriving through sustained nurturing.

Creating a gratitude jar is another effective way to strengthen this practice. This tangible method reflects nature's habit of storing resources, such as seeds or water, for future sustenance. By writing moments of gratitude on slips of paper and placing them in a jar, you symbolically store positive energy. Over time, jar fills, it becomes a reservoir of accumulated gratitude, reminding you of the wealth already present in your life. During periods of stagnation or low energy, much like times of drought in nature, revisiting the jar serves as a source of positivity, revitalizing your energy and reconnecting flow of abundance.

Establishing a daily gratitude ritual connects energy to the natural cycles of day and night. Just as the sun rises and sets, marking the passage of time, a gratitude practice at the start or end of each day mirrors this rhythm. Reflecting at dawn or sunset grounds your energy, much like the deep roots of a tree that provide stability in turbulent weather. Sharing this ritual, such as family or friends, extends its impact outward, creating a network of shared energy and support, akin to how plants share nutrients in an ecosystem to promote collective growth.

Mindfulness meditation further aligns gratitude with the natural Earth energies. Becoming present during meditation taps into the currents that sustain life, much like rivers flowing steadily toward the ocean. Focusing on gratitude during meditation allows for connect deeply with these energies, synchronizing your intentions with the natural processes that nourish growth. Visualizing the things that are appreciate while meditating enhances balance and focus, much like a tree standing tall through changing seasons by remaining anchored and centered.

Incorporating affirmations infused with gratitude amplifies their transformative power, functioning much like photosynthesis, where sunlight fuels growth in plants. Repeating affirmations like, "I am grateful for the abundance in my life," transforms positive energy into higher vibrations. This energetic shift strengthens your ability to manifest, much like light energizing a plant's development. By consistently using gratitude-infused affirmations, you provide intentions with the energy they need to flourish, aligning your personal growth with nature's cycle of expansion and abundance.

A gratitude collage or vision board extends this connection to nature's energy. Just as diverse ecosystems thrive through balance, gathering images alongwith words that reflect both appreciation and aspirations mimics how nature harmonizes various elements. Arranging these visuals as a representation for your goals reinforces the energy you wish to attract, much like the interdependence of species within a habitat fosters collective well-being.

Viewing your collage regularly strengthens the bond between your current reality and future dreams, supporting the manifestation process.

Expressing gratitude toward others mirrors the symbiotic relationships seen in nature, where cooperation along with mutual support foster growth. By showing appreciation through kind words, written notes, or thoughtful gestures, you nurture positive energy within your community. Just as trees in a forest share resources through interconnected root systems, gratitude fortifies the bonds between people, creating a high ripple effect of positivity. This shared energy amplifies abundance and reinforces the manifestation process, attracting more positive skills into your life.

Practicing gratitude for yourself is equally vital in harnessing nature's energy for manifestation. Just as ecosystems rely on self-sustaining cycles, such as plants replenishing soil nutrients, acknowledging your own strengths and growth is important. Recognizing achievements and celebrating efforts replenishes your internal energy reserves, aligning with the principle that what you nurture will thrive. This self-acknowledgment boosts confidence, enabling you to manifest desires with superior ease, much like a well-nourished tree producing abundant fruit.

Nature itself serves as a profound teacher of gratitude. Immersing yourself in natural settings such as gardens, forests, or coastal areas fosters a bottomless sense of connection to the world everywhere you. Expressing gratitude of beauty of nature aligns your energy with Earth's vibrations, reinforcing with sense of balance and abundance. Appreciating these natural wonders provides a limitless source of gratitude, continually fueling personal growth and supporting your manifestation efforts.

Random kindness acts reflect the principles of pollination in nature, spreading energy and positivity beyond yourself. Acts such as helping a neighbor or offering a kind word contribute to the positive energy flow, much like bees pollinating flowers to sustain growth. Each kind gesture has to create potential transformation, generating the ripple effect that enhances both your life and the others lives. This giving cycle and receiving mirrors nature's reciprocity, aligning your personal energy with the universe's abundant flow.

5.3 Transforming Challenges into Opportunities: Lessons from Nature's Resilience

Gratitude goes beyond a simple expression of thanks, serving transformative force that connects deeply with the cycles of growth, adaptation, and renewal found in nature. At its essence, gratitude shifts the perspective, akin to how the seasons change in harmony with the Earth's rhythms. By embracing gratitude, particularly during times of difficulty, we align with nature's capacity to transform adversity into growth opportunities. Just as trees strengthen their roots in response to wind, gratitude helps us reframe challenges as catalysts for personal development and manifestation, turning obstacles into stepping stones.

In moments of hardship, much like ecosystems enduring droughts or storms, it is natural to feel overwhelmed by negativity. However, gratitude like a light breaking through the clouds, illuminating the hidden lessons within those challenges. Instead of viewing difficulties as insurmountable, gratitude allows us to see their transformative potential, mirroring nature's ability to adapt and thrive under pressure. For instance, the loss of a job may initially seem devastating, but gratitude can shift the perspective to recognize it as a chance to pursue a more meaningful career path, similar to a forest regenerating with new growth after a fire.

The principles for Law of Attraction, which suggest that the energy that is emitted attracts similar energies, reflect the patterns observed in nature. Plants, for example, convert sunlight into energy through photosynthesis, drawing on life-sustaining forces to thrive. Similarly, practicing gratitude promotions our vibrational frequency, aligning us with positive energy that attracts abundance. Acknowledging small joys amidst hardship mirrors nature's ability to find balance and harmony within chaos. Consider someone facing health challenges: while the struggle is undeniable, gratitude for moments of support or progress creates a dual experience. This duality acknowledges the difficulty while opening space for healing and growth, akin to ecosystems restoring balance after a disturbance.

Transforming challenges through gratitude often begins with a shift in internal dialogue, much like how nature adapts to changing conditions. Negative thoughts can create a mental environment as barren as an arid landscape, but gratitude acts like rain, revitalizing and encouraging growth. A simple practice, such as custody a daily journal to note small blessings, plants seeds of positivity in the mind. Over time, these seeds take root and shift the focus from shortage to abundance, comparable to the transformation of a desert blooming after rainfall.

The effects of gratitude extend beyond the individual, influencing the broader network of connections that sustain us, much like the interdependence within ecosystems. Adopting a grateful mindset inspires others, fostering a community built on positivity and collaboration. In same way plants support one another through root systems or animals engage in mutualistic relationships, gratitude strengthens human bonds. For example, a workplace infused with gratitude creates an environment of cooperation and resilience, resembling a well-tended garden where collaboration supports growth. This collective energy amplifies well-being and fosters success, much as nature thrives through interconnected harmony.

Expressing gratitude also creates a reciprocal exchange of energy, similar to the relationship between pollinators and plants. Acts of gratitude, such as thanking someone or performing a kind gesture, reinforce connections and create a giving cycle and receiving. This mutual exchange mirrors flowers providing nectar to bees in return for pollination, fostering a belonging sense and shared purpose. During challenging times, these connections become essential. Simple acts of gratitude, whether verbal expressions or thoughtful actions, strengthen community ties and reveal the opportunities within shared adversity.

Gratitude fosters innovation by transforming challenges into opportunities, reflecting how ecosystems adapt to new conditions. Many significant breakthroughs, much like new ecological systems emerging after natural disturbances, are born from adversity. Nature constantly evolves, with trees developing thicker bark to resist fire or animals adapting to shifting climates. Similarly, gratitude helps us approach obstacles not as barriers but as chances to rethink and innovate. This perspective unlocks creativity and curiosity, enabling growth and adaptation much like nature's ever-evolving solutions.

CHAPTER 6

TAKING INSPIRED ACTION

6.1 The Balance Between Thinking and Doing: Nature's Rhythm of Creation

Law of Attraction often emphasizes the power of thoughts and intentions in bringing desires to life, but this is important to recognize the role of inspired action. This dynamic balance between thought and action reflects nature's processes, where growth, movement, and interaction with the environment are essential. Dreams and desires, much like seeds in fertile soil, require care and actionable effort to transform into tangible outcomes. Nature teaches while vision is crucial, the synergy of intention and action is what ultimately drives manifestation.

In nature, cycles of growth, decay, and renewal embody a harmony between stillness and transformation. Similarly, in manifestation, thoughts and intentions lay for groundwork, but like seeds germinating in soil, these ideas require active nurturing to grow. While thoughts act as sunlight, action serves as water, enabling desires to sprout and thrive. Without action, ideas remain potential, never transitioning into reality. Manifestation, much like the natural world, demands that dreams be met with proactive engagement to bring them to fruition.

Our beliefs, emotions, and intentions serve as unseen forces guiding the manifestation process, much like the Earth's natural elements shape its cycles. These thoughts resemble the currents of wind or the gravitational pull on tides, subtly influencing outcomes. Law of Attraction asserts that cultivating a positive, clear mindset aligns us with energy of our aspirations, mirroring how ecosystems adjust to environmental changes. However, without action, such thoughts remain abstract, ungrounded in the material world.

Inspired action parallels instinctual behaviors in nature, such as birds migrating or trees extending their roots. This type of action stems from intuition and alignment with one's higher purpose. Just as animals respond to environmental cues, inspired action arises when we tune in to our inner guidance, naturally leading us toward opportunities aligned with our goals. This process requires awareness, akin to how ecosystems adapt to shifting conditions.

Practices of meditation and mindfulness enhance this attunement, helping us discern the right moments to act or wait, much like the Earth anticipating rain.

Progress in nature often unfolds incrementally, such as rivers gradually carving through mountains. Similarly, inspired action not have to be grandiose; consistent small steps build momentum over time. Ecosystems evolve through slow, deliberate layering of biodiversity, and same way, breaking large goals into manageable actions makes them more achievable. Each small effort nurtures the larger vision, bringing it closer to reality, much like watering seeds allows them to bloom gradually.

The energy behind our actions profoundly influences their outcomes, just as the quality of sunlight and water affects plant growth. Actions driven by fear or desperation are like harsh environmental conditions that hinder development, whereas actions fueled by trust and enthusiasm flow effortlessly, supporting growth. Approaching goals with confidence and joy aligns our energy with the rhythms of creation, fostering opportunities and resources. This process mirrors healthy ecosystems that flourish over time through harmonious interactions.

Trust plays a fundamental role in both natural and manifestation processes. Just as seeds take time to sprout, desires need patience and faith in their eventual realization. Nature does not rush; instead, it unfolds for own pace, teaching us the value of trusting the process. Letting go of rigid control allows opportunities to arise organically, much like rivers adjusting to obstacles as they flow toward the sea. By releasing necessity for immediate results, we open ourselves to outcomes that may exceed expectations, delivered in perfect timing.

Setbacks are not failures but necessary steps for process of growth, much like disturbances in nature lead to renewal. Forests regrow stronger after wildfires, and similarly, challenges in our manifestation journey offer opportunities to learning and adaptation. Nature demonstrates that resilience is essential for thriving, and by reframing obstacles as lessons, we stay aligned with our goals. This perspective allows us to maintain momentum, just as a tree continues growing despite losing branches during a storm.

Feedback is invaluable in both nature and manifestation. Ecosystems constantly adjust based on environmental feedback, refining their processes for better harmony. Similarly, taking inspired action includes staying open to feedback, allowing us to adapt and refine our efforts in response to changing circumstances. This flexibility mirrors the adaptability of plants and animals, enhancing our alignment with universal energies. Attuning to feedback ensures that our actions remain purposeful and effective, bringing us nearer to our desires.

Collaboration and community are integral to both manifestation and nature. Just as ecosystems thrive through interdependence, so do we. Collaboration amplifies creative energy and brings diverse perspectives, akin to species within an ecosystem supporting one another. Surrounding ourselves with compatible individuals strengthens our motivation and creates a network of shared growth. Inspired action becomes a collective endeavor, where each person's success uplifts the group, much like the interconnected health of an ecosystem benefits all its members.

6.2 Recognizing Inspired Action: Nature's Intuitive Flow in Manifestation

The concept of Law of Attraction emphasizes the role of both thought and action in manifestation, with inspired action being the bridge that connects the two. Recognizing inspired action involves tuning into the subtle, instinctual nudges that align with goals and desires, much like the natural rhythms guiding ecosystems toward growth and harmony. Just as seeds sprout after rain or birds migrate in response to seasonal changes, inspired action arises from an intuitive connection to purpose, prompting you to move for harmony with your aspirations. It is an alignment of inner intention and outer action, akin to the tides responding to the moon's gravitational pull.

To identify inspired action, it is vital to develop awareness of your inner guidance system. This intuition often emerges when external distractions are quieted, much like how nature thrives in moments of stillness. The noise of daily life-technological distractions, societal expectations, or personal doubts-can obscure the subtle signals of inspiration. Practices like meditation, time spent in nature, or reflective journaling act as tools to clear this mental clutter, creating space for lucidity and connection. These stillness moments are like clearing a dense forest path, allowing intuitive insights to emerge. Inspiration often feels light, exciting, and compelling, akin to the first signs of spring heralding renewal and growth, and stands in contrast to the heaviness of fear or doubt.

In nature, all organisms function in agreement with their surroundings. Plants instinctively grow toward sunlight, rivers carve their paths through landscapes, and animals follow migratory patterns. Similarly, inspired action aligns thoughts, emotions, and behaviors natural flow of your goals. When you visualize your dreams and feel a sense of enthusiasm or hopeful anticipation, these emotions signal alignment. Inspired action feels like a gentle breeze nudging you forward, even if it pushes you beyond comfort zone. Just as plants must break through soil to reach sunlight, inspired action often requires you to step out of familiar patterns and take risks to fulfill your potential.

Inspired action manifest in various forms, ranging from small, incremental steps to significant, bold leaps. Growth in nature occurs in phases, from a seed's initial sprouting to a flower's full bloom, and similarly, inspired action often begins with small steps like seeking advice, validation up for a course, or visualizing a goal. These seemingly minor actions accumulate, much like raindrops nourishing the soil, eventually leading to significant opportunities. Synchronicities and spontaneous moments of inspiration often arise, guiding you toward your desires, much like a river winding its way to the sea through unexpected pathways.

The interconnectedness of nature aids as a reminder that inspired action is often amplified through community and collaboration. Just as ecosystems thrive through cooperation among plants, animals, and elements, human growth flourishes in supportive environments. Surrounding yourself with compatible individuals who encourage your aspirations creates a nutrient-rich environment for inspiration to flourish. Collaboration can spark fresh ideas and lead to new opportunities, much like how wind disperses seeds to create growth in new places. This collective energy acts as fertile soil, nourishing individual and shared growth.

Inspired action, like natural cycles, often needs patience and trust. Just as a tree takes time to bear fruit or a river carves its path over centuries, the manifestation process unfolds gradually. Each step, no matter the small, contributes to the larger journey. While progress may seem nonlinear or slow, every action serves a purpose in the grand design of your desires, much like the unfolding of seasons. Trusting the timing of the universe allows you to remain open to unforeseen outcomes and opportunities, fostering a sense of faith akin to trusting that spring will follow winter.

Gratitude plays a central role in recognizing and nurturing inspired action. Expressing appreciation for each step you take reinforces the flow of inspiration and attracts further opportunities. Gratitude shifts the perspective from lack to abundance, enhancing your ability to perceive and act upon inspiration, much like sunlight energizing plants for growth. By celebrating even the smallest victories, you signal for universe your readiness to receive more, creating a positive feedback loop where gratitude and inspiration fuel one another.

Self-compassion is equally important when taking inspired action. Nature shows us that not every seed will grow or every plant will thrive, yet growth and renewal continue. Similarly, not every action will lead to immediate success, and setbacks are fragment of the process. Practicing kindness toward yourself during moments of doubt or uncertainty fosters resilience, allowing you to continue forward. Like a forest recovering after a storm, self-compassion helps you recoil back from challenges and remain attuned to your intuition, understanding that the journey is as important as the destination.

Clarity improves your ability to recognize inspired action. When your goals and desires are clearly defined, it converts easier to discern which actions align with your vision. Just as rivers flow toward the ocean and the sun rises predictably each day, clarity of purpose acts as a scope, guiding you toward inspired steps that align with your true meanings. This sense of direction allows you to navigate your journey with confidence and purpose, much like how plants instinctively grow toward the light.

6.3 Building a Manifestation Action Plan: Cultivating Your Garden of Dreams

Creating a Manifestation Action Plan mirrors the process of cultivating a thriving garden, where every step contributes to the growth and flourishing of your dreams. Law of Attraction, much like nature's balance, relies on harmonizing thought and action. It's not sufficient to dream; your aspirations must be nurtured with deliberate steps. Each goal you set is akin to a unique plant, requiring its own care and environment to thrive, whether it's a profession goal symbolizing steady growth, relationships blooming like vibrant flowers, or personal fulfillment rooting deeply into your life. The important is to understand and provide what each intention needs to flourish.

Begin by clarifying your intentions, much like deciding what to plant in your garden. Reflect deeply on what you truthfully desire. Whether it's financial stability, emotional connections, or personal growth, every aspiration needs clear definition. Writing down these desires acts as the planting of seeds, anchoring your goals in the tangible world. Just as nature transforms seeds into saplings over time, putting your intentions into words connects your thoughts to the material world. This written record becomes a guidepost, offering clarity and focus as you progress.

Breaking down r goals into minor, actionable steps ensures steady progress. Just as nature's growth happens in stages-seasons bringing gradual change-your goals should be approached incrementally. Each step serves as a stepping stone, building momentum. For example, if financial independence is your aim, actions like saving a set amount monthly or researching investment opportunities resemble enriching the soil and preparing the conditions for growth. These small yet significant actions help for sense of accomplishment, much like observing a sapling grow taller with each passing day.

Prioritizing your goals is like determining which plants in your garden require the most immediate care. Focus on the aspirations that will create the greatest impact or hold the deepest meaning for you. As you work through these priorities, maintaining positive outlook. The energy you project, like sunlight and warmth, directly influences the manifestation process. Practices such as gratitude journaling are powerful tools for cultivating this positive energy. By acknowledging what you're grateful for, you shift from a mindset of scarcity to one of abundance, enriching your mental/emotional environment, much like nutrients fortify the soil.

Inspired action is a keystone of your manifestation action plan, mirroring nature's innate responsiveness. Intuitive nudges and synchronicities are like natural cues-the pull of roots toward water or the instinctive migration of birds. These signals often feel like moments of clarity or bursts of motivation, guiding you toward opportunities aligned with your desires. Trust these moments and action on them with confidence. They are your internal compass, much like nature's instinct to adapt and flow with changing conditions.

Maintaining momentum requires a daily routine dedicated to your goals, much like consistent care ensures the health of a garden. Incorporate practices such as visualization, meditation, or focused work on your tasks. These habits help sustain the energy needed for manifestation. Surrounding with supportive individuals creates a community of encouragement, akin to plants thriving in the interconnected ecosystem of a forest.

CHAPTER 7

REMOVING BLOCKAGES

7.1 Identifying Emotional Blockages - How nature do it

Identifying emotional blockages can be compared to uncovering the intricate root systems hidden beneath the earth's surface, revealing the knots and obstructions that hinder optimal growth. Just as a tree's roots may struggle against rocks or compacted soil, our emotional blockages arise from unresolved experiences, limiting beliefs, and fears that interrupt the energy flow essential for manifesting our deepest desires. In nature, a plant may fail to thrive due to unseen barriers below the surface; similarly, we encounter life's obstacles rooted within us. Embracing the principles of Law of Attraction have addressing these emotional roots to restore the smooth energy flow necessary for achieving our goals, akin to enriching the soil to nourish a flourishing plant.

These blockages often branch from past experiences, much like the rings of a tree reflect the impact of past storms. Early life events-rejections, criticisms, or fears-can plant seeds of self-doubt in the fertile soil of the mind. These seeds may grow into deep-rooted beliefs of inadequacy, much like invasive species overtaking a vibrant ecosystem and stifling its natural growth. To uncover such blockages, introspection becomes as vital as carefully examining soil for signs of imbalance. Tools such as journaling, much like documenting seasonal changes in a forest, allow us to articulate the subconscious patterns influencing our emotions. Writing our thoughts offers clarity, much like observing the stages of a plant's growth helps diagnose its health.

Fear frequently serves as a central force behind these blockages, including fears of failure, success, or vulnerability. In nature, fear can be likened to a frost that stunts development, preventing a plant from realizing its potential. As a gardener shields delicate seedlings from frost, we must recognize as well as address the ways fear freezes our emotional growth. Identifying cycles of self-sabotage resembles noticing recurring patterns in nature's cycles, enabling us to disrupt them and nurture our emotional wellness. This process requires courage, much like a seedling breaking through the soil toward sunlight, as discomfort often precedes the flowering of potential.

Negative self-talk is likened to weeds infiltrating a garden, consuming resources intended for flourishing plants. These internal voices are not inherent to our mental landscape; they resemble invasive species taking root over time. Cultivating mindfulness allows us to remove these negative thoughts, replacing them with affirmations that promote growth, much like restoring native plants to enrich the ecosystem. Techniques such as cognitive restructuring act as the gardener's tools, transforming thoughts like "I am not enough" into "I am worthy of success and growth." Just as tending a garden requires consistent effort, fostering a positive internal dialogue demands ongoing attention. Our internal energy, much like the condition of soil, directly affects what we can manifest. Emotional blockages diminish vibrational energy, akin to poor soil inhibiting plant growth. Practices like meditation, deep breathing, and yoga serve as nutrients that restore this energy, breaking through layers of resistance to reestablish balance. By engagement with these in these practices, we cultivate awareness of our internal needs, similar to a gardener assessing soil quality to foster healthy growth.

Emotional intelligence mirrors the symbiotic relationships within ecosystems, highlighting the interdependence and balance essential for resilience. This self-awareness enables us to identify our own emotional blockages and understand their impact on relations and environments. Much like a thriving ecosystem, emotional intelligence promotes healthier connections, fostering a environment for conducive to personal and collective growth. By strengthening emotional intelligence, we create the relational support necessary for achieving our aspirations, much like a well-tended garden fosters biodiversity.

Emotional blockages, while challenging, is also a opportunities for growth. Similar to how harsh weather conditions strengthen a plant's resilience, these blockages reveal areas in need of healing and reflection. By viewing these challenges as lessons, much like a gardener assesses a plant's recovery after a storm, we can better understand our needs and cultivate deeper self-awareness. This reframing transforms frustration into a inclination to learn, fostering growth through the healing process.

Self-compassion acts as the sunlight and water essential for overcoming emotional blockages and encouraging growth. Nature's patience with its cycles, allowing plants to bloom in their own time, reminds us to give ourselves with similar kindness. This compassionate perspective enables us to address emotional blockages without judgment, fostering the resilience desirable to persist through challenges. Just as a gardener creates a nurturing environment for plants, self-compassion provides the foundation for personal growth.

Support of a community functions much like the interdependent relationships within ecosystems. Plants thrive when surrounded by complementary species, and similarly, humans benefit from the encouragement of others. Whether through therapy, friendships, or group support, leaning on others can offer the insight and comfort needed to navigate emotional blockages. This collective strength mirrors how plants shelter each other from harsh winds, reminding us that shared growth is a influential tool in overcoming personal challenges.

Creative expression acts as a channel for exploring and releasing emotional blockages, akin to wildflowers bringing vitality to previously barren landscapes. Art forms such as writing, painting, or music allow emotions to flow freely, tapping into deeper layers of understanding. By expressing what words alone cannot convey, we release pent-up energy and find healing, much like a river clearing debris to reveal clear waters beneath.

7.2 Identifying and Clearing Emotional Blockages: Nature's Path to Manifestation

Identifying emotional blockages is an essential step in manifesting desires and effectively applying Law of Attraction. These blockages often stem from unresolved past experiences, limiting beliefs, and fears that disrupt the alignment of energy required for achieving goals. Just like a river's flow can be obstructed by rocks and debris, emotional blockages hinder the natural movement of energy toward one's aspirations. Addressing these blockages involves deep introspection, much like a gardener nurturing the soil to ensure healthy growth, to create a good foundation for clarity and manifestation.

Emotional blockages often originate from formative experiences, similar to how a tree's scars tell stories of past storms. Experiences of rejection, criticism, or fear can plant seeds of self-doubt, which grow into entrenched beliefs of unworthiness, much like invasive species overtaking a vibrant ecosystem. These beliefs manifest as hesitation or avoidance in pursuing goals. Introspective practices, such as journaling, help individuals uncover how these past events shape current emotions and decisions. Journaling acts as a instrument for documenting emotional patterns, much like recording seasonal changes in nature, allowing individuals to gain insight into their internal landscape.

Fears also play a significant role in forming emotional blockages. Fear of failure, success, or vulnerability functions like frost, stunting growth before it begins. This fear creates cycles of self-sabotage, where individuals unconsciously reinforce limiting beliefs. For example, a terror of failure might lead someone to procrastinate, much like a vine hesitating to climb a trellis. Recognizing these patterns requires courage and self-awareness, akin to pruning a tree to encourage healthier growth. Facing these fears is uncomfortable but necessary for emotional and personal progress.

Negative self-talk acts like weeds in a garden, crowding out the positive thoughts essential for growth. These internal voices often arise from societal pressures or personal experiences, creating a cycle of doubt and inadequacy. To address this, cultivating awareness and challenging the validity of negative beliefs is essential. Cognitive restructuring transforms harmful thoughts into positive affirmations, such as reframing "I am not good enough" to "I am capable of achieving my goals." This process mirrors replacing invasive weeds with native plants that enrich an ecosystem. Consistent practice helps dismantle negative thought patterns, clearance the path for aligned energy and manifestation.

Emotional blockages also affect vibrational energy. Law of Attraction emphasizes that like appeals like; negative emotions repel desired outcomes, much like poor soil conditions inhibit plant growth. Processing and releasing these emotions through mindfulness meditation, deep breathing, or yoga raises vibrational frequency, akin to enriching soil to nurture vibrant growth. These practices foster emotional awareness and provide tools for navigating internal challenges, much like a planter tending to each plant's unique needs.

Developing emotional intelligence enhances the ability to identify and address blockages. Emotional intelligence is comparable to understanding the interconnected relationships within an ecosystem, enabling individuals to recognize how their emotions impact themselves and others. This awareness fosters healthier interactions and a helpful environment for personal growth, much like a balanced ecosystem sustains diverse life forms.

While challenging, emotional blockages are valuable opportunities for growth. Just as disturbances in nature can lead to resilience and biodiversity, emotional challenges reveal underlying issues and unmet needs. For instance, feelings of unworthiness may stem from unresolved childhood experiences. Addressing these blockages is akin to classifying and addressing the origin cause of soil infertility. By viewing tests as opportunities for growth, individuals adopt a constructive mindset, empowering themselves to heal and move forward.

Practicing self-compassion is crucial when addressing emotional blockages, much like how plants thrive with patience and care. Self-compassion creates a nurturing environment for emotional exploration, allowing individuals to confront fears without judgment. This attitude fosters resilience and self-acceptance, creation it easier to address and clear blockages, much like how a gardener gently tends to delicate plants.

Community support also plays an invaluable role, reflecting the symbiotic relationships in ecosystems where mutual support enhances growth. Connecting with others through therapy, support groups, or friendships provides validation and insight, offering new perspectives on challenges. Sharing experiences can illuminate hidden paths for healing, much like how interconnected plant species strengthen an ecosystem.

Creative expression offers a therapeutic way to explore and release blockages. Writing, painting, or music allows individuals to express emotions non-verbally, similar to how animals use movement or song to communicate. Creative activities help uncover and process deep-seated feelings, much like a river clearing debris to reveal its flow. Engaging in artistic endeavors facilitates emotional release and fosters a deeper connection with one's inner self, open the way for greater clarity and alignment.

Addressing emotional blockages requires patience and commitment, much like nurturing a garden to fruition. It is a transformative journey involving discomfort but ultimately leads to greater position with one's desires. By clearing these blockages, individuals unlock their potential to manifest their goals, much like a forest regenerating stronger after a fire. This process offers profound rewards, including clarity, purpose, and fulfillment, akin to the flourishing of a well-tended garden.

Proactively addressing emotional blockages with tools such as workshops, courses, or self-help resources equips individuals with strategies for growth. These resources deliver new insights into overcoming challenges, empowering individuals to shape their emotional landscape much like gardeners actively cultivate their gardens. Setting clear intentions is another powerful practice, aligning thoughts and emotions with goals and acting as a road for manifestation. This practice highlights emotional barriers, much like planning a garden reveals which plants require more sunlight or shade.

7.3 Forgiveness: Nature's Essential Cycle in Manifestation

In the intricate manifestation process, forgiveness emerges as a critical component, functioning much like nature's cyclical rhythm of releasing and renewing. Within the framework of Law of Attraction, forgiveness mirrors the natural process of growth and letting go, acting as a mechanism to shed emotional burdens that impede the stream of positive energy. Much like trees release their leaves in autumn to make space for new growth, forgiveness enables individuals to release resentment, anger, and hurt, creating an environment for healing and fresh opportunities. Nature's inherent rhythm demonstrates that letting go is essential for renewal, and this principle applies directly to the inner journey of positioning with one's desires.

Often misunderstood as weakness or passive acceptance, forgiveness is, in truth, an act of profound strength. Just as rivers overcome obstacles by finding ways to flow around them, forgiveness redirects emotional energy toward freedom and growth. It is not about excusing harmful actions but liberating oneself from the weight that obstructs progress. Harboring negative emotions is akin to stagnant water in a marsh, cutting off the flow of vibrant energy needed for manifestation. This stasis blocks the transformative energy of new possibilities, much like a forest struggling to thrive without adequate sunlight.

The weight of unresolved emotions becomes a significant obstacle, manifesting as stress, anxiety, and even physical symptoms. These blockages resemble overgrown brambles preventing forward movement, or a garden overtaken by weeds that stifle growth. To clear these barriers, individuals must confront and release unresolved feelings, akin to tilling soil and removing obstructions to create a productive environment for growth. Practices like journaling, meditation, and self-reflection serve as tools to externalize and process emotions, much like a gardener prepares the ground to nurture healthy plants.

Forgiveness is deeply interconnected with self-love and self-acceptance, providing the foundation for growth. Plants need light and nourishment to thrive, just as individuals require compassion to flourish. Resentment directed inward acts like overcrowded roots stifling a plant's development. Learning to forgive oneself for past mistakes provides the emotional space necessary for new growth, enabling a profounder sense of self-compassion. This process resembles a plant receiving the care and attention it needs to expand and bloom, transforming self-directed anger into a source of personal strength.

The principles of Law of Attraction operate on the idea that like appeals like, a concept mirrored in nature's harmonious ecosystems. Resentment and anger emit a vibrational energy that resonates with negativity, much like certain environmental conditions can attract destructive elements. By forgiving, individuals shift their frequency from one of bitterness to one of healing and abundance. This vibrational elevation aligns them with positive energies that encourage growth and transformation, similar to how a balanced ecosystem fosters diversity and harmony.

Forgiveness does not require forgetting or condoning harm, much like nature acknowledges and absorbs the energy of a storm without denying its impact. Instead, it involves releasing the hold these experiences have on one's life. Forgiveness allows for acknowledgment and processing, followed by forward movement, much like a river cleansing itself after a storm. Journaling, meditation, along mindfulness help facilitate this process, serving as tools to externalize turmoil and prepare for renewal, much like planting seeds in freshly tilled soil.

Setting boundaries is an essential part of forgiveness, reflecting nature's need for space to thrive. Trees flourish when given adequate room, and individuals grow stronger when they establish emotional boundaries that safeguard their well-being. Forgiving does not mean continued engagement with harmful influences; rather, it involves protecting one's energy while releasing resentment. This balance ensures that personal growth continues, much like a tree sheds weak branches to focus its energy on healthier growth.

As individuals embrace forgiveness, they often experience a profound shift, similar to how a forest flourishes after a cleansing rain. Releasing emotional blockages invites a surge of new energy, fostering improved relationships, opportunities, and inner peace. This shift mirrors the sunlight breaking through clouds, encouraging new growth and revitalizing the landscape. The internal transformation brought about by forgiveness radiates external, to create a ripple effect that touches all aspects of life.

Forgiveness also strengthens gratitude, a cornerstone for manifestation, much like the symbiosis of sun, rain, and soil sustains life. Letting go of resentment allows individuals to appreciate the present moment more fully, akin to plants thriving under optimal conditions. Gratitude raises vibrational frequencies, amplifying the ability for attract abundance. This cycle of forgiveness and gratitude mirrors a well-tended garden, where the harmonious interplay of care and appreciation nurtures growth and vitality.

Visualization techniques can amplify the process of forgiveness, much like a gardener envisioning a flourishing garden before planting seeds. Imagining the release of pain and the flow of constructive energy creates a mental and emotional shift, akin to the first sprout breaking through the soil. Paired with affirmations centered on self-love and compassion, visualization reinforces the commitment to let it go and embrace growth, mirroring nature's endless capacity for renewal.

Mindfulness further supports the practice of forgiveness, much like a farmer's attentive care ensures healthy crops. By staying present, individuals can recognize when they are holding onto negativity and consciously choose to release it, akin to pulling weeds before they overtake a garden. Mindfulness fosters a compassionate response to life's challenges, creating an emotional environment where forgiveness and manifestation thrive.

CHAPTER 8

THE ROLE OF ENERGY AND VIBRATION

8.1 The Rhythm of Energy Frequencies: Tuning into Nature's Vibrations for Manifestation

Understanding energy frequency is central to the principles of Law of Attraction and manifestation, emphasizing that everything in existence-our thoughts, emotions, and surroundings-vibrates with energy. This energy, like the natural beats of the tides or the cycles of the seasons, flows in patterns and resonates at unique frequencies. By aligning ourselves with higher energy frequencies, akin to how plants harmonize with the cycles of sunlight and rain, we can influence the realities we manifest. This principle reveals the interconnectedness of our inner states and external experiences, much like the interplay of elements in nature that sustain life and growth.

Energy frequency refers to the rate at which energy vibrates, similar to how a river flows with varying intensity or wind moves through trees. All matter, thoughts, and emotions possess vibrational frequencies that determine their interaction with surrounding energies. Higher frequencies, associated with emotions like love, gratitude, and joy, resemble the uplifting sun warmth in spring. Conversely, lower frequencies, linked to fear, anger, or despair, can be likened to storm clouds disrupting harmony. Law of Attraction functions through this principle: like interests like. When we emit high-frequency energy, we attract corresponding positive experiences, much like how flourishing ecosystems draw life and diversity.

This idea of vibrational energy finds resonance in quantum physics, which demonstrates the fluid and interconnected nature of the universe. Quantum theories reveal that particles existed in multiple potential states until observed, underscoring the idea that our focus and energy shape our reality. Like rivers carving through mountains or wind sculpting landscapes, our emotions and thoughts influence the route of our lives. By consciously cultivating high-frequency emotions, we align with the flow of possibility, altering our experiences to reflect the energy we project.

Our thoughts/emotions act as signals, sending vibrational frequencies into the universe, akin to how the Earth reflects and absorbs sunlight. Negative thoughts and limiting beliefs generate low-frequency energy, obstructing the manifestation process, much like a shadow blocking light. Conversely, cultivating positive emotions such as gratitude and hope raises our frequency, allowing us to appeal abundance and joy. This dynamic interplay mirrors the balance of natural ecosystems, where equilibrium fosters vitality. Just as nature thrives through harmonious interactions, we must regulate our inner states for manifest our desires.

Gratitude is one of the most effective practices for elevating energy frequency, functioning like sunlight that nourishes life. By appreciating the current moment, we align with abundance, much like how nature aligns with the cycles of growth and renewal. Expressing gratitude shifts focus from lack for abundance, creating a vibrational match with the outcomes we wish to manifest. Scientific studies underscore gratitude's ability to enhance happiness alongwith life satisfaction, mirroring how optimal conditions in nature lead to flourishing ecosystems. This practice generates a feedback loop where gratitude attracts more reasons for appreciation, reinforcing a high-energy state conducive to manifestation.

Meditation, mindfulness, and visualization are additional tools for raising energy frequency, akin to natural processes that restore balance and clarity. Meditation calms the mind, much like a still lake reflecting its surroundings, fostering peace and attunement to higher vibrations. Mindfulness anchors us in the present, helping shift focus from undesirable to positive states, akin to observing the subtle transitions between seasons. Visualization acts as a blueprint for creation, enabling us to connect emotionally with our goals as though they are already realized. This process mirrors the way seeds carry the full prospective of the plants they will become, channeling energy toward growth and fulfillment.

Our external environment significantly influences energy frequency, much like how the health of an ecosystem depends on its conditions. Negative surroundings can drain energy, pulling us into lower vibrations, much like barren landscapes struggle to sustain life. Positive environments-whether uplifting relationships, inspiring content, or serene spaces-nurture high-frequency states, resembling the fertile soil that supports a thriving garden. By curating supportive surroundings, we reinforce our vibrational alignment with desired outcomes, much as a gardener ensures optimal conditions for growth.

Energy frequency extends beyond the individual to collective consciousness, resembling the interconnectedness of ecosystems. When individuals raise their vibrations through positivity and compassion, they contribute to a ripple effect, fostering greater harmony and abundance on a broader scale. Like a solitary seed growing into a tree that supports countless forms of life, individual efforts to elevate energy frequency can inspire widespread transformation. This collective shift toward higher frequencies mirrors the balance and cooperation found in nature, where each element contributes to the whole.

8.2 Raising Your Vibrational State: Nature's Path to Manifestation

Acknowledging the intricate connections within existence, elevating one's vibrational state stands as a central aspect of the manifestation process, comparable to how a flower instinctively turns toward sunlight in pursuit of sustenance. To fully harness the supremacy of Law of Attraction and actualize aspirations, it is important to understand that all living entities, including humans, are composed of energy. Each individual emits a distinctive vibrational frequency-a unique energetic resonance influenced by their thoughts, emotions, and actions. This vibration intertwines with the earth energies, sky, and water, shaping the realities individuals encounter. By raising vibrational energy, one aligns with frequency of their aspirations, akin to a rising tide lifting a river, drawing it closer to its ultimate destination. This practice, deeply rooted in self-awareness, mirrors how trees adapt to seasonal shifts, intuitively discerning when to grow, release, or rest.

Much like seasonal transitions bring changes in weather patterns, an individual's vibrational frequency fluctuates in response to internal states. The foundational step in enhancing this energy lies in cultivating self-awareness, developing an acute sensitivity to personal thoughts, feelings, and the energy emitted. Just as a forest floor must be cleared of accumulated debris to encourage growth, individuals must rid their minds of the clutter that anchors them to lower frequencies. Persistent negative thoughts, entrenched limiting beliefs, and unprocessed emotions resemble stagnant water, stifling renewal and growth. Elevating vibrational energy necessitates acknowledging these restrictive patterns and actively choosing to transcend them, similar to a plant striving toward the nurturing embrace of sunlight.

Nature exemplifies mindfulness, offering lessons in embracing the present moment, much like mountains silently witnessing the passage of time. By practicing mindfulness, individuals synchronize with nature's steady rhythms, silencing distractions to become attuned to their internal processes without judgment. Observing emotions as transient, like clouds drifting across the sky, fosters awareness of their impermanence. In embracing this stillness, individuals discern negative thought designs that inhibit progress, akin to clearing underbrush in a thriving forest. Replacing these patterns with affirmations-positive declarations of intention-is comparable to planting seeds. With time as well as consistent nurturing, these seeds flourish, substituting scarcity with abundance, fear with love, and doubt with trust. Simple affirmations such as "I am deserving of life's beauty" serve to raise one's vibrational state, much as rain enriches the earth, enabling life to flourish.

Gratitude emerges as a transformative tool for raising vibrational energy, aligning individuals with nature's constant cycles of giving. Gratitude mirrors sunlight breaking through after rainfall, illuminating life's gifts often overlooked. Practicing gratitude is comparable to tending a garden, requiring sustained attention to life's inherent beauty. A gratitude journal becomes a means of honoring daily miracles, akin to a gardener nurturing newly sprouted plants. By acknowledging life's blessings, individuals cultivate a productive environment for abundance to take root. Expressing gratitude toward others deepens interpersonal connections, elevating collective energy, much like how interconnected tree roots support the entire forest ecosystem.

Pure joy represents one of the highest attainable frequencies. Connecting with sources of joy aligns individuals with nature's effortless rhythms, similar to a river flowing naturally along its course. Nature encourages finding joy in simplicity-the melody of birdsong at dawn, the sensation of grass underfoot, or the warmth of sunlight. Engaging in actions that ignite happiness elevates energy, creating an open invitation for further joy. Whether walking amidst trees, engaging in creative expression, or sharing laughter, moments of joy resemble fleeting spring blossoms-transformative despite their brevity. As the earth alternates between growth, rest, and renewal, individuals must regularly carve out space for joy to bloom, enriching their vibrational energy.

The physical body, inherently connected to the earth's energy, profoundly impacts vibrational frequency. Consuming fresh, nutrient-rich foods imbued with the sun's energy parallels nourishing soil with rain to sustain plant life.

Staying hydrated resembles feeding a tree's roots, promoting energy flow throughout the body. Movement, whether through dance, yoga, or a simple walk in nature, invigorates the body, elevating its energy. The body's vitality, akin to a balanced ecosystem, thrives when nurtured. By honoring physical needs, individuals enhance their energy flow, raising vibrational frequency, much like a bird soaring upward on a favorable wind current.

Meditation, akin to sitting beside a tranquil pond, quiets the attention and fosters clarity. This practice facilitates alignment with higher universal vibrations, echoing the rhythmic meeting of ocean waves with the shore. Visualization, a meditative technique, holds particular power in manifestation. Visualizing desires as though already realized creates an energetic blueprint, much like a tree's innate orientation toward sunlight. Consistent meditation and visualization practices maintain connection to one's highest self, inviting universal energies to align with and support the manifestation of one's dreams.

Relationships, much like ecological systems, influence overall vibrational balance. Thriving forests depend on diverse, mutually supportive species, and similarly, relationships have a capacity to elevate or diminish energy. Surrounding oneself with persons who uplift and inspire fosters growth, akin to sunlight encouraging plant vitality. Conversely, draining relationships resemble invasive species encroaching on a garden's balance, necessitating the establishment of boundaries or severance. By cultivating positive connections and protecting personal energy, individuals sustain their vibrational arrangement with their highest intentions.

Self-care encompasses tending to the inner garden of the soul. Plants require sunlight, water, and conducive environments for growth, just as individuals need nurturing for emotional and spiritual well-being. Engaging in restorative activities-whether a peaceful forest walk, reading, or quiet reflection-bolsters vibrational energy. This care extends to self-dialogue, where words act as seeds within consciousness. Speaking kindly to oneself cultivates a garden of self-love. Transforming negative self-talk into affirmations, akin to pruning dead branches, allows space for new growth.

The environments individuals create mirror their inner states, resembling ecosystems in the ability to nurture or hinder energy. A decluttered, organized space parallels a well-tended garden, permitting energy to flow unobstructed. Introducing elements that inspire-beautiful artwork, natural materials, or soothing scents-imbues spaces with positivity. These environments, as extensions of individual energy, harmonize with elevated vibrations, fostering alignment between surroundings and aspirations.

8.3 The Energy of Surroundings: A Natural Connection to Manifestation

In the dynamic interplay of life, energy serves as the invisible thread weaving through all things-plants, rivers, animals, and the very air around us. To truly harness the art of manifestation, one must grasp the significance of energy along vibration, much like understanding how sunlight sustains an entire forest ecosystem. The energy we radiate through our thoughts, emotions, and actions resonates with the universe, creating ripples that shape our reality. This principle is ancient in origin yet affirmed by modern quantum physics, which reveals that all matter, including ourselves, is composed of vibrating energy.

In the natural world, energy is in perpetual motion, a constant exchange that mirrors the energy flowing through human experiences. Consider the wind rustling through a meadow or waves lapping at the shore-these forces are reminders of life's dynamic vibrations. Our environments, both physical and emotional, significantly influence our energy. Whether it's the spaces we inhabit, the relationships we nurture, or the content we consume, these external elements interact with and shape our personal vibrations. Much like how an ecosystem thrives or deteriorates based on its balance, so too does our energy fluctuate with our surroundings.

The environments we create reflect our internal state and, in turn, influence how we feel and act. A cluttered room, with objects scattered like debris after a storm, can impede the flow of energy, fostering stagnation and overwhelm. Conversely, clean, organized, and light-filled space resembles a thriving sunlit forest, alive with possibilities. By mindfully organizing and maintaining our surroundings, akin to a gardener pruning plants, we cultivate spaces that inspire and align for aspirations. This alignment creates fertile ground where intentions can flourish, much like seeds taking root in nutrient-rich soil.

Relationships, too, play the pivotal role in shaping our energy. Just as trees in a forest grow stronger when surrounded by healthy companions, we thrive when connected to uplifting and supportive individuals. Every person carries a unique vibration, and these energies merge during interactions. Positive relationships act as nourishing sunlight, enriching our spirits, while toxic or negative relationships resemble invasive vines, sapping vitality. To maintain high vibrations, it's essential to nurture connections that elevate and distance ourselves from those that drain, much like treatment to a garden to remove weeds and allow flourishing growth.

Nature itself serves as a profound source of energy alignment and healing. Its seamless rhythms provide a blueprint for harmonizing our own energy. Walking through a forest, listening to the rustle of leaves, or feeling the cool touch of water against the skin helps recalibrate our energy, much like rain revitalizing parched soil. Immersing ourselves in nature connects us to the universe's higher frequencies, grounding and elevating us simultaneously. Regularly spending time outdoors strengthens this connection, aligning our personal vibrations with the natural harmony that fuels manifestation.

Our digital environments, much like physical ones, influence the vibrational state. In today's fast-paced digital age, the content we engage with is akin to the diverse elements within an ecosystem. Positive, inspiring content serves as a meadow of flourishing flowers, whereas fear-driven or divisive material mirrors polluted streams, dragging down our energy. Mindfully curating what we consume online protects our vibrational frequency, allowing it to flow freely and align with desires. By seeking uplifting, enriching content, we foster an energetic state conducive to growth and manifestation.

Physical health is intimately tied to energy. Just as plants draw sustenance from the soil and sunlight, our bodies thrive on what we consume and how we move. Nutrient-dense, fresh foods cultivated from the earth act as fuel, raising our energy much like the sun nourishes plant life. Movement, whether through dance, yoga, or simple walks in nature, mimics the graceful flow of animals through forests, releasing pent-up energy and restoring balance. Caring for our bodies, much like nurturing an ecosystem, ensures a harmonious energy flow that boosts our vibrational state and enhances manifestation potential.

Gratitude acts as a influential amplifier for raising vibration. Much like the sun's rays transforming the earth after a storm, gratitude shifts focus for lack to abundance. Expressing thankfulness, whether through a journal gratitude or daily affirmations, strengthens our connection to life's inherent gifts, allowing us to align higher frequencies. This practice acts like deep roots anchoring a tree, drawing nourishment from the moment of present. By consistently cultivating gratitude, we create an energetic foundation where intentions can take shape, much like a well-tended garden bursting into bloom.

CHAPTER 9

MANIFESTING RELATIONSHIPS AND ABUNDANCE

9.1 Manifesting Healthy Relationships: Tapping into Nature's Rhythms of Connection

In the intricate web of life, the dynamics of healthy relationships mirror the harmony of natural ecosystems. Just as every organism in nature contributes to a balanced environment, relationships thrive when energies are aligned in mutual respect and understanding. Law of Attraction teaches that the energy we emit, akin to the gentle sway of trees in the breeze, shapes the connections we attract. Manifesting meaningful and nurturing relationships requires harmonizing our inner energy with love, trust, and respect, much like the symbiotic bonds that sustain nature.

The journey to healthy relationships begins with self-awareness and inner reflection, comparable to a tree rooting deeply into the earth before its branches can flourish. Our past experiences and beliefs, like the soil supporting a tree, shape the foundation of our connections. Emotional baggage-unresolved hurts or limiting beliefs-can stifle growth, much like a tree conserves energy by shedding old leaves in winter. Acknowledging and releasing these burdens through introspection or journaling clears the way for healthier connections, akin to pruning withered branches to encourage new growth.

Self-love forms the fertile soil from which all healthy relationships sprout. When we nurture and value ourselves, like a flower turning toward the sun, we radiate an energy that attracts others who respect and cherish our worth. Acts of self-love-whether through creative expression, nature walks, or quiet meditation-mirror the steady, nourishing flow of a river. Regular self-care replenishes the soul, cultivating a vibrant energy field that draws kindred spirits, much like wildflowers draw pollinators with their fragrance.

Visualization is the powerful tool for manifesting relationships, much like envisioning a lush landscape before planting a garden. Imagining your ideal connection in vivid detail-the shared laughter, mutual respect, and moments of understanding-creates an emotional blueprint. This practice, like nurturing a seedling, sets the foundation for something lasting and beautiful. Visualization works best when infused with clarity and intention, helping align your energy with the relationships you seek.

Clear intentions act as the roots anchoring your desires in reality. Writing down the qualities you value in a partner or friendship solidifies your vision, much like planting seeds in well-prepared soil. While maintaining focus, it's vital to remain open to unexpected outcomes, much like a field of wildflowers bends and adapts with the wind. Trusting the universe to guide the right connections into your life fosters an atmosphere of possibility, ensuring your relationships evolve naturally.

Gratitude is a transformative force in cultivating healthy relationships, akin to rain nourishing the earth. Acknowledging and appreciating the connections you already have shifts your focus from scarcity to abundance, creating fertile ground for more relationships to flourish. By maintaining a daily gratitude practice, you elevate your vibrational frequency, much like a tree thriving in well-nourished soil. Expressing gratitude for the love and support around you attracts even more positive connections, reinforcing the cycle of abundance.

Healthy communication forms the lifeblood of strong relationships, much like nutrient exchanges in the soil sustain life. Honest and open dialogue fosters trust and understanding, inviting deeper connections. Vulnerability, akin to a flower slowly opening to sunlight, encourages others to connect on a genuine level. Authentic communication attracts individuals who value sincerity, creating bonds rooted in mutual respect.

Boundaries are essential for healthy relationships, serving as natural markers of balance, much like rivers carve their banks or forests grow in harmony. These boundaries define where your energy ends and another's begins, enabling both independence and connection. Articulating your needs and respecting others' ensures relationships flourish without overextension, much like ecosystems maintaining equilibrium to allow all species to thrive.

Letting go of control is integral to manifesting healthy relationships, akin to rivers flowing naturally toward the sea. Relationships are dynamic, evolving over time. Trusting the universe to guide your connections, without forcing outcomes, fosters growth and authenticity. Just as nature follows its rhythms, each relationship brings unique lessons and growth opportunities, regardless of its duration.

9.2 Attracting Financial Abundance: Aligning with the Natural Flow of Prosperity

Attracting financial abundance is a process deeply intertwined with understanding and aligning with the natural energy flows of the universe. Much like tending to a garden, this practice requires introspection, nurturing, and a harmonious balance between intention and action. Law of Attraction teaches that the energy we emit-shaped by our beliefs, emotions, and thoughts-guides the flow of abundance or scarcity into our lives, much as a river follows the path of least resistance.

Our internal beliefs about money are the roots of our financial reality. To manifest prosperity, one must examine these beliefs, much like a gardener assessing the quality of soil before planting seeds. Past experiences and societal conditioning often plant limiting beliefs that block the flow of abundance, akin to debris obstructing a river's flow. Journaling emotions about money helps uncover these blockages. For instance, feelings of unworthiness, guilt, or fear of wealth can create energetic barriers. Recognizing these patterns allows for clearing and healing, much like removing weeds to allow water and nutrients to reach the roots of plants.

Replacing limiting beliefs with empowering affirmations is the next step, akin to planting new seeds in fertile soil. Affirmations such as "I am deserving of financial prosperity" or "Wealth flows to me effortlessly" shift the energy from lack to abundance. Just as sunlight nourishes a growing plant, repeating these affirmations daily nurtures the mindset needed to attract financial blessings.

Visualization acts as a powerful tool to align energy with the reality of abundance. Imagining oneself in a state of financial prosperity, much like envisioning a flourishing garden, creates an emotional resonance with that reality. Vividly picturing the life you desire-your ideal home, experiences, and financial security-aligns your frequency with the vibrations of abundance. Consistently engaging in this practice deepens the connection, much like watering a sapling to ensure its steady growth.

Gratitude is an essential practice, akin to the rain that nourishes the earth. Expressing thankfulness for the financial blessings already present in your life elevates your vibrational frequency, creating fertile ground for more abundance. Maintaining a gratitude journal to acknowledge financial gifts-whether large or small-reinforces an attitude of abundance. Expressing gratitude for future financial prosperity, as though it has already arrived, further strengthens this energetic alignment.

Manifestation also requires action, much like a river carving its path through the landscape. Inspired actions-whether pursuing a new job opportunity, starting a side business, or investing in skills-signal to the universe your readiness to receive abundance. These steps, though sometimes small, create momentum and reinforce your alignment with financial prosperity. Trusting your intuition and taking consistent steps mirrors the persistence of nature's processes, where every small effort contributes to growth.

The energy of your surroundings also plays a crucial role in shaping your financial reality. Much like how plants thrive in the right environment, your financial growth depends on being in uplifting spaces and engaging with supportive individuals. Decluttering your home and workspace clears stagnant energy, making room for abundance to flow. Surround yourself with people who inspire and encourage you, as their energy supports your vibrational alignment.

Money, like water, is a flowing resource, and embracing its natural rhythm is essential. Practicing generosity-whether through acts of kindness, donations, or sharing resources-aligns you with the principle of circulation. Just as seeds scattered by the wind lead to new growth, sharing wealth with joy and purpose attracts prosperity back to you in unexpected and meaningful ways.

Patience is another lesson nature imparts. Just as a seed does not become a tree overnight, manifesting financial abundance requires trust in the process. While the results may not be immediate, every small step contributes to the larger picture. Engage in fulfilling activities that maintain your energy alignment, trusting that the universe is working in your favor, even when progress seems slow.

9.3 Creating a Supportive Community – Nature path for growth

Creating a supportive community plays a pivotal role in manifesting healthy relationships and abundance, acting as a collective energetic space where shared goals and positive intentions thrive. This concept transcends mere social interaction, focusing instead on fostering mutual growth, shared values, and encouragement. When like-minded individuals come together, their energies amplify, much like an ecosystem flourishing through interdependence. This heightened vibrational frequency makes it easier to align with the principles of Law of Attraction, ultimately enabling the manifestation of shared and individual desires.

The energy of those around us significantly impacts our own. Every person we interact with contributes their unique vibrational frequency to our environment, influencing whether our energy is elevated or diminished. Surrounding ourselves with individuals who share our aspirations and inspire us enhances our vibrational state, creating a ripple effect of positivity. For example, joining a group dedicated to practicing Law of Attraction strengthens belief systems and fosters a shared sense of motivation. The collective energy within such a group becomes a driving force, propelling everyone toward their goals with greater momentum.

Deep, meaningful connections form the foundation of a supportive community. These relationships thrive on vulnerability, empathy, and a safe space for open expression. In such an environment, individuals feel empowered to share their victories and struggles without fear of judgment. This openness fosters trust and mutual respect, creating a network of encouragement where members can confidently pursue their goals. Knowing that support is always available allows individuals to focus on their manifestations, free from the burden of fear or doubt.

A supportive community also provides access to shared knowledge and resources. Every member brings unique insights, skills, and experiences that enrich the collective wisdom. Sharing stories of success and lessons learned from challenges allows individuals to gain new perspectives and strategies for achieving their own goals. For instance, one member's experience in manifesting financial abundance can serve as a roadmap for others. This exchange of ideas not only broadens individual horizons but also strengthens the group's overall capacity for growth and manifestation.

Accountability is a key benefit of a supportive community. When individuals share their intentions and goals within the group, a sense of responsibility develops, motivating them to take consistent action. Regular check-ins, collaborative challenges, and shared milestones reinforce this accountability, creating a culture of persistence and mutual encouragement. Knowing that others are invested in one's success provides the extra push needed to stay committed, even when faced with obstacles.

Collaboration within a community accelerates progress toward abundance by pooling collective resources, such as knowledge, skills, and networks. This collaborative spirit fosters a sense of belonging and solidarity, aligning with the idea that abundance grows when shared. For instance, one person's professional connections might open doors for another, while someone else's advice on personal growth could inspire new approaches. Supporting each other's goals creates a dynamic cycle of giving and receiving, where every contribution elevates the group as a whole.

Diversity within a community enriches the collective experience by introducing a variety of perspectives and approaches. Engaging with individuals from different backgrounds encourages creativity, open-mindedness, and flexibility in pursuing goals. This diversity fosters dynamic growth, helping individuals discover new pathways to success that they might not have envisioned on their own. A community that celebrates differences becomes a fertile ground for innovation, respect, and collective empowerment.

The energy contributed to a community is as vital as the energy received from it. Approaching interactions with positivity, support, and a genuine willingness to listen nurtures a space where everyone can flourish. By engaging with the intent to uplift and empower others, we elevate the community's vibrational frequency, creating an environment conducive to manifestation. Conversely, negative energy can stifle growth, emphasizing the importance of kindness, collaboration, and encouragement in all interactions.

CHAPTER 10

COMMON MISCONCEPTIONS

10.1 Debunking Myths About Law of Attraction: Unveiling Nature's Principles of Manifestation

The principles of Law of Attraction and manifestation, celebrated as transformative tools, are often misunderstood due to prevalent misconceptions. These myths can hinder effective use of these concepts, much like a gardener struggling to grow plants without understanding the soil's needs. To truly benefit from Law of Attraction, it's important to address these misunderstandings and align one's approach with the deeper truths behind the process.

One of the most common misconceptions is the idea that mere positive thinking can bring about desired outcomes without effort. While positivity can uplift the spirit, Law of Attraction requires a harmony of thoughts, emotions, and actions, much like how a plant needs both sunlight and water to thrive. Visualization along with affirmations are essential, but they must be coupled with concrete steps toward achieving goals. For example, improving health involves visualizing vitality while also exercising and maintaining a nutritious diet, reflecting the balance of intention and action found in nature's cycles.

Another myth is the belief that Law of Attraction functions as a transactional process: simply ask the universe, and your desires will materialize. This oversimplifies the nuanced interaction of energies required for manifestation. The process is not about making demands but about aligning your internal state-your beliefs, emotions, and intentions-with your aspirations. This alignment mirrors the adaptability of ecosystems, which respond dynamically to environmental shifts. For example, attracting love requires nurturing self-love and cultivating an openness to connection, harmonizing one's energy with the relationships they wish to create.

The idea that manifestation allows one to passively wait for results is another widespread misunderstanding. Manifestation demands inspired action, akin to the effort of a seed breaking through the soil to reach sunlight. Visualization and belief are vital, but proactive steps are necessary to bring desires to fruition. For instance, aspiring entrepreneurs must not only envision success but also develop business plans, network, and seek out resources, just as nature's processes require effort and persistence.

A common source of disillusionment is the belief that Law of Attraction guarantees success. Like nature's unpredictability, the manifestation process doesn't always yield the exact outcomes imagined. However, these unexpected results can often lead to greater fulfillment or clarity about one's true desires. Flexibility and openness to change are essential, allowing the universe to guide individuals toward what serves them best, even if it diverges from their original vision.

Another myth presents Law of Attraction as a quick fix for life's problems. This oversimplification neglects the deeper emotional work often required for meaningful change. Manifestation, much like tending a garden, involves addressing and resolving limiting beliefs and past wounds. Preparing the internal environment for manifestation ensures that desires can take root and flourish authentically, much like enriching the soil before planting seeds.

The misconception that Law of Attraction is solely about material gain limits its transformative potential. While many use it to manifest wealth and success, its principles extend to fostering relationships, personal growth, health, and spiritual alignment. A singular focus on material outcomes can overshadow the profound personal evolution and joy that arise from aligning with one's highest self and purpose.

Another harmful belief is that any negative thought or emotion will derail manifestations. This creates pressure to maintain constant positivity, which is neither realistic nor healthy. Law of Attraction encourages the acknowledgment and constructive processing of negative emotions rather than their suppression. Emotional balance is akin to nature's cycles, where storms and rain nourish the earth, clearing the way for new growth.

The notion that Law of Attraction operates through mystical or illogical means is another misunderstanding. While there is a spiritual dimension, its principles are rooted in psychological truths. Our thoughts shape our perceptions and behaviors, which in turn influence our outcomes. This alignment of mindset, behavior, and energy is supported by cognitive psychology, emphasizing that a practical and open approach enhances the manifestation process.

10.2 The Difference Between Manifestation and Wishful Thinking: Nurturing Intentions in Nature's Garden

Manifestation and wishful thinking often seem similar on the surface, but they differ profoundly in principles, methods, and outcomes. Manifestation is a deliberate, proactive process requiring clarity, action, and emotional alignment, whereas wishful thinking is a passive approach, relying on hope without corresponding effort. Understanding these distinctions is essential to effectively harness the power of manifestation, much like cultivating a thriving garden requires intention, care, and effort.

Manifestation involves intentionally creating a desired reality by aligning thoughts, emotions, and actions with specific goals. It mirrors nature's rhythms, where growth results from both intention and nurturing. For instance, someone manifesting a new career doesn't merely visualize success; they take tangible steps, such as applying for jobs, networking, and developing relevant skills. In contrast, wishful thinking is passive, rooted in the hope that desires will materialize without effort. A wishful thinker may long for a healthier lifestyle but fail to adopt habits like regular exercise or balanced nutrition, neglecting the essential action required for transformation.

A key difference between the two lies in addressing underlying belief systems. Manifestation emphasizes identifying and transforming limiting beliefs that can obstruct progress. For example, someone aspiring to financial abundance may uncover internal narratives like "I'm not good with money" and replace them with affirmations such as "I am capable of managing wealth effectively." This alignment between conscious intentions and subconscious beliefs strengthens the manifestation process. Wishful thinking, by contrast, tends to overlook these deeper beliefs, focusing on surface-level desires without resolving internal conflicts that hinder progress.

Gratitude is another defining feature of manifestation. Practicing gratitude shifts focus from lack to abundance, fostering an environment where desires can flourish. By appreciating current blessings, individuals align themselves with the frequency of abundance, creating fertile ground for manifestation. Wishful thinking often fixates on what's missing, reinforcing a scarcity mindset that stifles growth. Gratitude, like nutrient-rich soil, enriches the manifestation process, providing a strong foundation for desired outcomes.

Patience and trust are vital components of manifestation, recognizing that results unfold in alignment with natural timing. Just as plants grow through gradual cycles, manifestation requires consistent effort and faith in the process. Wishful thinking, on the other hand, is often tied to immediate gratification, leading to frustration when outcomes aren't instantaneous. Manifestation encourages patience and resilience, teaching individuals to trust the journey rather than becoming discouraged by delays.

Visualization is the powerful tool in manifestation, but its application differs significantly from the fleeting daydreams of wishful thinking. Manifestation involves vividly imagining desired outcomes with emotional and sensory detail, creating an energetic alignment with those goals. This practice is coupled with purposeful action, reinforcing the belief that the vision is attainable. Wishful thinking, however, lacks this structured approach, relying on fantasies disconnected from actionable steps or emotional alignment.

Manifestation acknowledges the importance of external factors and synchronicities, emphasizing a co-creative process between the individual and the universe. While individuals work to align internally, they must also remain open to opportunities, connections, and external influences that support their goals. Wishful thinking often ignores this interplay, expecting results to occur in isolation. Manifestation recognizes that external circumstances can catalyze progress, much like environmental factors influence the growth of plants.

Emotional alignment is central to manifestation, as the energy emitted through emotions shapes what we attract. Manifestation encourages cultivating emotions such as joy, gratitude, and confidence, which elevate vibrational energy and strengthen the ability to manifest desires. Wishful thinking often stems from a place of lack or negativity, creating energetic blocks that hinder progress. Manifestation teaches that maintaining a positive emotional state amplifies the manifestation process, much like sunlight nourishes growth in nature.

Manifestation also emphasizes resilience in the face of challenges. The journey is rarely linear, and obstacles are seen as opportunities for growth and learning rather than failures. Manifestation encourages individuals to adapt and persevere, akin to how plants grow stronger in response to environmental pressures. Wishful thinking, by contrast, may falter in the face of adversity, as it lacks the proactive mindset needed to overcome setbacks.

Self-awareness further distinguishes manifestation from wishful thinking. Manifestation requires a deep understanding of one's intentions, motivations, and values, ensuring that goals resonate with the individual's authentic self. This introspection fosters clarity and purpose, aligning desires with long-term fulfillment. Wishful thinking often skips this reflective process, focusing on superficial wants without considering their deeper significance or alignment with personal values.

10.3 Understanding the Limits and Potential of Manifestation: Nurturing Growth in Nature's Cycle

Law of Attraction and manifestation, while widely discussed, are often misunderstood, with numerous misconceptions distorting their essence and potential. Understanding these principles with clarity involves debunking myths and embracing a holistic, nuanced approach. This deeper perspective mirrors nature's complexity, where growth, balance, and timing all play interconnected roles.

A common misconception is that manifestation relies solely on positive thinking. While maintaining a positive mindset is important, it is not sufficient on its own. Manifestation requires intentional action to accompany positive thoughts, aligning beliefs and behaviors with desired outcomes. For instance, someone aiming for career success must visualize their goals and also take practical steps such as acquiring relevant skills, networking, and actively seeking opportunities. This integration of thought and action reflects nature's harmony, where both sunlight and water are needed for plants to grow.

Personal responsibility and self-awareness are pivotal in manifestation. It's not simply about desiring an outcome but also examining internal factors such as subconscious beliefs that may contradict your intentions. For example, someone seeking financial stability may unknowingly harbor limiting beliefs about money, such as associating wealth with greed or feeling unworthy of abundance. These hidden blocks act like weeds in a garden, stifling growth until they are identified and removed. Addressing these beliefs transforms the foundation of manifestation, creating fertile ground for success.

Another myth is that manifestation yields instant results. In today's fast-paced world, it's tempting to expect immediate outcomes, but manifestation, like nature, unfolds gradually. Seeds take time to germinate, and flowers bloom in their season. Similarly, the journey of manifestation requires patience, persistence, and trust in the process. Challenges and setbacks are not failures but opportunities for growth and refinement, encouraging deeper alignment with one's goals.

Manifestation also does not occur in isolation from one's environment. External circumstances, such as economic conditions, societal influences, and interpersonal relationships, shape the manifestation process. Recognizing these factors helps set realistic expectations and fosters a proactive approach. For instance, an artist aspiring to success must cultivate their craft while navigating industry challenges, much like a gardener tending the soil to support growth. Awareness of these external dynamics enhances manifestation by integrating effort with context.

The role of community in manifestation is often overlooked. While manifestation is deeply personal, surrounding yourself with supportive, like-minded individuals amplifies your energy and intentions. Collective energy, like an interconnected ecosystem, strengthens the manifestation process, providing encouragement and shared resources. A supportive community acts as fertile soil, nurturing individual aspirations and fostering collective growth.

Manifestation is frequently misunderstood as purely materialistic, but its scope extends far beyond acquiring wealth or possessions. True manifestation involves aligning with one's higher self and pursuing a life rich with purpose and meaning. Material goals, such as financial success, are often stepping stones toward deeper aspirations, such as providing for loved ones or contributing to meaningful causes. Shifting focus from superficial gains to intrinsic motivations deepens the manifestation journey and enhances fulfillment.

It's important to recognize that manifestation is not a guarantee of success. External factors like timing, opportunity, and chance influence outcomes. While Law of Attraction helps align thoughts and actions with goals, life's unpredictability means that not all desires will manifest as envisioned. This does not indicate failure but reflects the dynamic nature of growth, much like how ecosystems adapt to changing conditions. Flexibility and resilience are essential, allowing individuals to navigate unexpected paths toward fulfillment.

Gratitude is a foundational element in manifestation, often underestimated. Practicing gratitude shifts focus from lack to abundance, elevating vibrational energy and inviting positive outcomes. Gratitude acts like sunlight on a thriving garden, nourishing the manifestation process. By appreciating current blessings, individuals create a fertile environment for their desires to flourish, reinforcing a cycle of positivity and abundance.

CHAPTER 11

DEVELOPING A PERSONAL PRACTICE

11.1 Creating Your Daily Manifestation Routine: Cultivating Growth in Nature's Rhythm

Creating a daily manifestation routine is an intentional and structured way to align your thoughts, emotions, and actions with your goals, much like cultivating a well-tended garden to encourage growth. The process involves clear goal-setting, mental practices, and consistent actions that, when combined, create a fertile environment for your desires to materialize.

The step first is defining your goals. Reflect on what you truly wish to achieve across various aspects of your life, such as career, relationships, health, or personal fulfillment. Writing these goals in detail provides clarity and direction, much like planting seeds in well-prepared soil. This act not only organizes your intentions but also strengthens your connection to them, ensuring your focus remains unwavering.

Visualization is the powerful practice to include in your routine. Set aside quiet time each day to mentally immerse yourself in the reality of your goals being achieved. Close your eyes and vividly picture the desired outcome, engaging all your senses to make the experience feel tangible. Imagine the sights, sounds, emotions, and even scents associated with your manifested goals. This process reinforces the connection between your intentions and the energy of realization, akin to sunlight nurturing young plants.

Affirmations are another cornerstone of manifestation routines. These positive statements reprogram your subconscious mind to support your goals, counteracting self-doubt and negativity. Select affirmations that align with your desires, such as "I attract success effortlessly" or "Abundance flows freely to me." Repeat them daily with conviction, either out loud or silently, ensuring you truly believe in their truth. Over time, these affirmations act as consistent nourishment, much like water sustaining a thriving plant.

Incorporating gratitude into your practice helps shift your mindset from scarcity to abundance, raising your energy to attract more positive experiences. Each day, note three to five things you are grateful for, focusing on both small and significant blessings. Gratitude amplifies your awareness of existing abundance, creating an energy field that attracts further prosperity, similar to how a flourishing ecosystem thrives when nurtured.

Meditation is essential for centering your energy and creating mental clarity. Regular meditation, whether through breathwork, mindfulness, or guided sessions, helps calm the mind, release limiting beliefs, and connect with your intuition. This stillness fosters inner alignment, allowing inspired thoughts and actions to emerge naturally, much like the harmony found in balanced natural environments.

Setting daily intentions directs your focus and energy. Begin each morning by declaring what you aim to achieve or embody for the day, such as "I will seize opportunities that support my growth" or "I intend to remain confident and focused." These intentions act as guideposts, ensuring that your actions remain aligned with your goals.

Adapting your routine as needed is also vital. Life's dynamics may shift, and your aspirations may evolve. Periodically reassess your goals and adjust your practices to ensure they reflect your current path. This flexibility mirrors how trees adapt to their surroundings, ensuring steady and resilient growth.

Your environment significantly influences your manifestation efforts. Cultivate a space that inspires positivity and focus, keeping it clean, organized, and filled with items that uplift your spirit. Consider creating a vision board with images, affirmations, and symbols that represent your desires, placing it somewhere visible to keep your intentions front and center. This visual representation acts as a constant reminder of your goals, much like the vibrant colors of a blooming garden energize its caretaker.

Taking inspired action is a non-negotiable part of the manifestation process. While mental practices like visualization and affirmation are crucial, real-world steps are equally important. Inspired action involves following your intuition and proactively pursuing opportunities that align with your goals. Whether it's learning new skills, connecting with others, or taking calculated risks, these steps bridge the gap between intention and realization, much like how a seed actively grows toward the light.

Consistency is the backbone of any manifestation routine. Dedicate time each day, whether a few minutes or an hour, to engage in your practices. Consistency signals commitment to your desires and builds momentum, even on days when motivation wanes. Small, steady efforts accumulate over time, much like consistent rainfall nurtures a thriving garden.

11.2 Tools and Resources for Continuous Growth: Nurturing Your Manifestation Garden

Developing a personal routine focused on Law of Attraction and manifestation is crucial for anyone seeking to use their thoughts and intentions to influence reality. This discussion highlights various tools and techniques that can promote consistent growth in the journey to manifest your aspirations. While Law of Attraction is widely recognized, integrating effective practices into daily life can profoundly enhance results. Each method serves a specific role, helping align your mind, emotions, and actions with your deepest goals.

A key strategy in building a manifestation practice is visualization. This technique involves crafting detailed mental images of your desired outcomes, engaging the mind to believe in possibilities and potential success. Through visualization, you immerse yourself in a sensory experience-seeing, feeling, and hearing the emotions tied to achieving your aspirations. This process not only solidifies your intent but also sends strong vibrations into the universe, attracting conditions that align with your vision. Dedicate time daily to quiet reflection, closing your eyes to vividly picture your dreams. The more specific and lifelike the visualization, the stronger its impact on your subconscious, similar to how sunlight fosters the growth of a seedling.

Affirmations are another cornerstone for ongoing progress in manifestation. These positive statements help reprogram your subconscious by replacing limiting beliefs with empowering ones. Regularly repeating affirmations aligned with your goals creates a supportive mental environment. For example, affirmations like "I am deserving of endless opportunities" foster a sense of self-worth and alignment. Repeating them with emotion and conviction strengthens their effect. Writing affirmations in a journal or displaying them prominently keeps them top of mind, akin to maintaining consistent care for a plant to ensure its growth.

Meditation also plays an essential role in fostering clarity, peace, and focus-qualities vital for manifestation. This practice calms mental noise, connects you to your inner self, and opens pathways to intuitive insight. Meditation helps release negative emotions or blockages that hinder progress, much like roots burrow deep into the soil to find nourishment. Regular meditation enhances alignment with your true desires and supports manifestation through mindfulness, guided meditation, or self-love practices. These approaches can reduce stress while fostering emotional and mental alignment.

Journaling is another powerful tool that supports self-reflection and growth. Writing down thoughts, feelings, and experiences clarifies what you wish to manifest. A manifestation journal allows you to express your goals, track progress, and practice gratitude for your current circumstances. Writing helps release emotional blocks and negative patterns, paving the way for new opportunities. Reviewing past entries can provide valuable insights and help refine your approach, much like a gardener assessing a plant's health.

Vision boards are creative, tangible ways to keep your aspirations in focus. These visual tools represent your desires, offering a daily reminder of your intentions. Constructing a vision board involves gathering inspiring images, quotes, and materials related to your goals. The process itself is meditative, focusing your energy on what you wish to attract. Position your vision board where you'll see it often, keeping your desires vivid in your mind, much like the vibrant blooms of a well-tended garden.

Surrounding yourself with supportive individuals is another key aspect of this practice. The energy of those around you can significantly influence your thoughts and emotions, either propelling you forward or holding you back. Cultivating relationships with like-minded people who share your interest in Law of Attraction fosters encouragement and accountability. Participating in discussions, workshops, or online communities creates a sense of shared purpose, amplifying motivation and commitment. Positive energy from others strengthens your resolve to continue your practice.

Educating yourself about manifestation and Law of Attraction enhances your ability to apply these principles effectively. Reading books, attending workshops, listening to podcasts, or engaging in courses broadens your perspective and introduces fresh techniques. Learning from experienced practitioners provides practical strategies and deepens your understanding. The journey of manifestation is continuous, with each new insight further refining your approach and expanding your capacity to achieve your goals.

Gratitude is a transformative practice that can elevate your vibrational frequency and strengthen your manifestation efforts. Expressing gratitude shifts your focus from scarcity to abundance, creating a mindset that attracts more of what you appreciate. Start or end each day by listing things you're thankful for, whether small or significant. Gratitude cultivates positivity, aligns your energy with abundance, and creates fertile conditions for your aspirations to materialize, similar to how nutrient-rich soil supports healthy plant growth.

Inspired action is a non-negotiable component of manifestation. While thoughts and emotions set the foundation, action bridges intention and reality. Inspired action arises from intuition and alignment with your goals. Pay attention to opportunities that resonate with your intentions and take bold steps when necessary. This might mean pursuing new projects, networking, or learning new skills. Trust your instincts and be ready to step out of your comfort zone, much like a plant reaching toward the light to grow.

Accountability serves as a motivator in your manifestation journey. Sharing your goals with someone you trust creates a sense of commitment and support. Whether it's a friend, coach, or mentor, discussing your progress and challenges fosters clarity and encouragement. Accountability partners can keep you focused and provide valuable insights, reinforcing your dedication to the process.

Emphasizing self-care is vital for sustaining a manifestation practice. Caring for your physical, emotional, and mental well-being provides a solid foundation for effective manifestation. Activities such as exercise, eating well, and getting adequate rest enhance energy levels, while self-reflection and relaxation rejuvenate your spirit. Prioritizing self-care cultivates balance, creating a state of alignment conducive to manifesting your desires.

Incorporating rituals into your daily routine can enhance focus and intention. Rituals serve as symbolic acts that reinforce your commitment to Law of Attraction. Whether lighting a candle, reciting affirmations, or engaging in specific meditative practices, rituals create a sense of sacredness and intention. They signal to the universe your readiness to receive and provide a consistent anchor for your manifestation efforts.

Addressing limiting beliefs is essential for removing barriers to success. Negative thoughts often operate subconsciously, preventing progress. Identifying and challenging these beliefs can lead to profound transformations. Replace limiting beliefs with empowering alternatives to create space for growth, much like removing weeds to allow plants to thrive.

Patience and persistence are key virtues in manifestation. Results may not come immediately, but consistent effort and belief in the process ensure steady progress. Celebrate small successes along the way, as they signify movement toward your goals. Trust that the universe is aligning to support your journey and remain open to unexpected opportunities and lessons.

11.3 Building a Community of Like-Minded Individuals: Cultivating Connections for Manifestation

Building a community of individuals who resonate with your journey of mastering Law of Attraction and manifestation is a transformative step. This supportive network enhances your ability to align with your desires and manifest your goals by fostering a positive, uplifting environment. When surrounded by like-minded individuals, the energy and encouragement shared within the group amplify intentions, creating a collective force that propels everyone toward success.

Begin by reflecting on your core goals and values. Ask yourself: What do I want to manifest? Whether you seek abundance, creativity, health, or spiritual growth, understanding these aspirations helps you recognize individuals who share similar visions. Awareness of the energetic gaps in your current relationships can motivate you to connect with others through platforms like social media, workshops, or local meetups focused on manifestation practices.

Online platforms such as Facebook, Reddit, and Instagram offer dedicated groups and forums for manifestation enthusiasts. These virtual spaces allow for the exchange of experiences, tips, and success stories, fostering a sense of belonging and support. By actively participating in discussions, sharing your journey, and seeking advice, you can form connections that contribute to your growth and keep you motivated.

Workshops, seminars, and meetups provide opportunities for face-to-face interactions, enabling a more profound energetic exchange. Participating in activities like group meditations, intention-setting sessions, or informal discussions fosters accountability and collaboration. The collective energy of these gatherings uplifts all members, creating a powerful environment for manifestation.

Spiritual retreats, holistic fairs, and wellness events are excellent venues for meeting individuals on similar paths. Engaging with diverse perspectives enriches your understanding of manifestation and may lead to long-term connections that inspire and support your journey. Sharing insights and learning from others in these settings deepens your practice and strengthens your commitment.

Approach relationships within your community with authenticity and vulnerability. Sharing both triumphs and challenges creates a supportive atmosphere where members feel encouraged to pursue their goals without fear of judgment. Being open about your journey fosters trust and strengthens bonds, allowing the community to thrive as a collective unit.

Contributing to your community is equally important for maintaining its energy and effectiveness. Whether by organizing group activities, sharing personal experiences, or offering support, your involvement reinforces the group dynamic. Giving back to the community ensures a reciprocal flow of energy, benefiting everyone involved.

Be mindful of the energy you allow into your space. While compassion is essential, maintaining boundaries with individuals who drain your energy or disrupt the positive dynamic of the group is crucial. Protecting your vibration ensures that your manifestation practice remains aligned and effective.

Regularly engaging in shared rituals or activities, such as group intention-setting or collaborative vision board creation, can amplify the manifestation process. These collective practices focus energy on shared goals, creating a ripple effect that enhances the power of individual intentions. Celebrating each other's achievements within the community reinforces positivity and inspires continued progress.

CHAPTER 12

SELF-LOVE AND POSITIVE ENERGY

12.1 Cultivating Self-Love and Embracing Positive Energy: A Journey Within and Beyond

Self-love involves recognizing and valuing one's inherent worth, accepting one's unique identity, and embracing both strengths and imperfections. It is a practice of treating oneself with kindness, compassion, and understanding, particularly during challenging times or moments of failure. Much like a gardener who diligently tends to their plants to ensure they thrive, self-love requires consistent effort and self-reflection to nurture and maintain emotional well-being.

When individuals cultivate self-love, they build emotional resilience, akin to the deep roots of a tree that enable it to withstand powerful winds. Nature's cycles of growth and renewal offer profound lessons: just as the changing seasons rejuvenate the earth, self-love demands ongoing care and renewal to flourish. This practice fosters a flow of positive energy that enhances one's perspective on life while also contributing to a nurturing and supportive atmosphere for those around them.

The relationship between self-love and positive energy is comparable to the harmony of elements within an ecosystem. By embracing self-love, individuals replace negative self-talk and limiting beliefs with affirmations of self-worth and capability. This shift is reminiscent of the way sunlight, rain, and nutrients collectively sustain a plant's growth. A person grounded in self-love is more likely to face life with gratitude, optimism, and enthusiasm, creating a ripple effect that positively impacts relationships and social interactions..

12.2 Practical Approaches to Nurture Self-Love and Positive Energy

There are several ways to actively cultivate self-love and foster positive energy:

Mindfulness and Self-Reflection: Mindfulness practices encourage individuals to become aware of their thoughts and feelings without judgment. Self-reflection provides clarity, helping individuals understand their inner dialogue and make conscious choices to foster acceptance and compassion. Journaling is a helpful tool to express feelings and recognize patterns that may be holding one back, like a tranquil lake reflecting the sky above.

Setting Boundaries and Protecting Energy: Self-love involves knowing one's limits and protecting one's energy. Setting healthy boundaries in relationships and commitments ensures that individuals prioritize their well-being, much like how plants develop natural defenses against harmful influences. This practice reduces stress and fosters a sense of control over one's life.

Nurturing the Mind and Body: Replacing negative self-talk with affirmations can dramatically shift one's mindset. Affirmations, like "I am deserving of love and happiness," provide the positive light that nurtures the inner garden. Engaging in activities that bring joy, such as hobbies or passions, further reinforces self-love. Additionally, taking care of the body through nutrition, exercise, and adequate rest is vital to promoting energy and vitality, as the body is a vessel deserving of care and respect.

Surrounding Oneself with Positivity: Relationships built on mutual respect, understanding, and encouragement create a nurturing ecosystem where individuals can thrive. Just as trees in a forest are interconnected through their roots, humans too can create supportive connections that foster growth and resilience.

12.3 Overcoming Challenges and Embracing the Ripple Effect of Self-Love

The path to self-love is often met with obstacles stemming from societal pressures, past experiences, and ingrained negative conditioning. Overcoming these barriers requires recognizing and challenging societal norms that wrongly equate self-love with arrogance, as well as addressing deep-rooted beliefs formed by past traumas or mistakes. This process is akin to removing weeds from a garden, where healing and self-forgiveness are necessary steps to cultivate a thriving environment for self-love to grow.

Gratitude serves as a powerful tool in fostering self-love and positive energy. By shifting focus to the aspects of life for which one feels thankful, individuals move from a mindset of scarcity to one of abundance. Much like a gardener admiring each bloom, practicing gratitude strengthens the bond between self-love and positive energy. This reinforces a positive self-image and encourages further acts of self-care, creating a cycle of nurturing and growth.

30-DAY'S

LAW OF ATTRACTIONAND MANIFESTATION PLAN

WEEK 1: CLARITY AND MINDSET

Focus: Clarity of Desire, Shifting Mindset, Building Foundation

Day 1: Set Intentions and Get Clear

- Write down the specific things you want to manifest (career, relationships, health, etc.).

- Make sure they are specific, measurable, and clear.

- Example: Instead of "I want a better job," say "I am manifesting a career in marketing that allows me to work remotely and earn $80,000 a year."

Day 2: Journal About Your "Why"

- Write about why these desires are important to you.

- Connect emotionally to your desires and explore how achieving them will improve your life.

Day 3: Visualize Your Desired Life

- Spend 10-15 minutes visualizing your ideal life with your desires already manifested.

- Engage all your senses-see, hear, feel what it's like to live your dream life.

Day 4: Create Affirmations

- Write down 3-5 affirmations that align with your desires.

- Repeat them throughout the day, especially in front of a mirror.

- Example: "I am worthy of abundance, and opportunities flow effortlessly to me."

Day 5: Identify Limiting Beliefs

- Write down any limiting beliefs you have about your ability to manifest your desires.

- Replace each limiting belief with an empowering one.

Day 6: Gratitude Practice

- Start a gratitude journal.

- Write down 3 things you are grateful for every morning. This will help shift your mindset to focus on abundance.

Day 7: Meditation and Reflection

- Do a 10–15-minute guided meditation focused on clarity and manifestation.
- Reflect on your first week-how are you feeling about your goals? Are you noticing any mindset shifts?

WEEK 2: VISUALIZATION AND AFFIRMATION FOCUS

Focus: Deepening Visualization, Strengthening Affirmations

Day 8: Create a Vision Board

- Gather images, quotes, and words that represent your desires.
- Spend time putting together a vision board and place it where you will see it every day.

Day 9: Deep Visualization

- Dedicate 15 minutes to deeply visualize one specific aspect of your desired life.
- Focus on small details and experience the emotions as if it is already happening.

Day 10: Strengthen Your Affirmations

- Repeat your affirmations out loud with emotion, and write them down 10 times in your journal.
- Reinforce them by telling them every time you look in the mirror.

Day 11: Connect with Your Future Self

- Write a letter from your future self, imagining you've already achieved your goals.
- Describe what your life looks like, how you feel, and what you've learned.

Day 12: Gratitude for the Future

- Write 3-5 things you are grateful for in advance, as like desires have already manifested.
- Example: "I am so grateful for my new job and the joy it brings to my life."

Day 13: Guided Meditation for Manifestation

- Listen to a guided manifestation meditation that aligns your energy with your desires.

Day 14: Celebrate Small Wins

- Reflect on any small wins or shifts you've experienced.
- Write about how these are signs that you are on the right path.

WEEK 3: INSPIRED ACTION AND MOMENTUM

Focus: Taking Inspired Action, Building Momentum

Day 15: Plan and Act

- Identify 1-2 actions you can take that align with your desires.
- Example: If manifesting a new job, update your resume or apply for one position.

Day 16: Revisit Your Vision Board

- Spend time looking at your vision board and visualizing your desires.
- Feel the emotions that come up as like dreams have already been fulfilled.

Day 17: Affirmations While Moving

- Go for a walk or exercise and repeat your affirmations out loud or in your mind.
- Embody the energy of success and abundance.

Day 18: Seek Out Opportunities

- Be open to signs and opportunities that come your way.
- Take one inspired action today that moves you closer to your goals.

Day 19: Celebrate Your Progress

- Take time to acknowledge how far you've come.
- Write down any synchronicities or moments of alignment you've experienced.

Day 20: Create a Manifestation Ritual

- Develop a small ritual (light a candle, set intentions) that you can perform daily to enhance your practice.
- Use this time to focus on your intentions.

Day 21: Group Visualization

- If possible, join a group meditation or visualization session (online or in-person).
- Share your goals with like-minded individuals to amplify collective energy.

WEEK 4: ELEVATING ENERGY AND TRUST

FOCUS: ELEVATING ENERGY, SURRENDER, AND TRUST

Day 22: Practice Gratitude Throughout the Day

- Throughout the day, practice spontaneous gratitude. Every few hours, pause and mentally list 3 things you're grateful for at that moment.

Day 23: Tune Into Your Emotions

- Be mindful of how you feel during the day.
- When negative emotions arise, pause, acknowledge them, and consciously shift your focus back to gratitude or joy.

Day 24: Scripting
- Write out a "day in your life" as like desires have already manifested.
- Be detailed about how your day goes, how you feel, and what you're doing.

Day 25: Let Go and Surrender
- Reflect on your desires and release any attachment to how and when they manifest.
- Trust that the universe is aligning circumstances for you.

Day 26: Inspired Action 2.0
- Take one bold inspired action today.
- Example: Sign up for a new class, reach out to a potential mentor, or take a step toward something that scares you.

Day 27: Amplify Your Affirmations
- Record yourself saying your affirmations with confidence.
- Play them back to yourself and feel the power of your words.

Day 28: Group Energy
- Share one of your manifestations with a supportive friend or community.
- Discuss your progress and feel the support of like-minded individuals.

Day 29: Raise Your Vibration
- Do something today that makes you feel joyful and abundant.
- This could be dancing, spending time in nature, or engaging in a hobby that makes you feel alive.

Day 30: Review and Celebrate
- Reflect on the last 30 days.
- What has changed in your mindset, emotions, or experiences? Write down your successes, no matter how small.
- Celebrate your journey and trust that more is on its way.

www.ingramcontent.com/pod-product-compliance
Lightning Source LLC
LaVergne TN
LVHW031243190726
843493LV00010B/3000